AF782873

BUSINESS ECONOMICS IN A RAPIDLY-CHANGING WORLD

PRIVATIZATION

POLICIES, DEVELOPMENTS AND CHALLENGES

BUSINESS ECONOMICS IN A RAPIDLY-CHANGING WORLD

Additional books in this series can be found on Nova's website under the Series tab.

Additional e-books in this series can be found on Nova's website under the eBooks tab.

BUSINESS ECONOMICS IN A RAPIDLY-CHANGING WORLD

PRIVATIZATION

POLICIES, DEVELOPMENTS AND CHALLENGES

AMELIA HANSEN
EDITOR

nova publishers
New York

Copyright © 2016 by Nova Science Publishers, Inc.
All rights reserved. No part of this book may be reproduced, stored in a retrieval system or transmitted in any form or by any means: electronic, electrostatic, magnetic, tape, mechanical photocopying, recording or otherwise without the written permission of the Publisher.

We have partnered with Copyright Clearance Center to make it easy for you to obtain permissions to reuse content from this publication. Simply navigate to this publication's page on Nova's website and locate the "Get Permission" button below the title description. This button is linked directly to the title's permission page on copyright.com. Alternatively, you can visit copyright.com and search by title, ISBN, or ISSN.

For further questions about using the service on copyright.com, please contact:
Copyright Clearance Center
Phone: +1-(978) 750-8400 Fax: +1-(978) 750-4470 E-mail: info@copyright.com.

NOTICE TO THE READER

The Publisher has taken reasonable care in the preparation of this book, but makes no expressed or implied warranty of any kind and assumes no responsibility for any errors or omissions. No liability is assumed for incidental or consequential damages in connection with or arising out of information contained in this book. The Publisher shall not be liable for any special, consequential, or exemplary damages resulting, in whole or in part, from the readers' use of, or reliance upon, this material. Any parts of this book based on government reports are so indicated and copyright is claimed for those parts to the extent applicable to compilations of such works.

Independent verification should be sought for any data, advice or recommendations contained in this book. In addition, no responsibility is assumed by the publisher for any injury and/or damage to persons or property arising from any methods, products, instructions, ideas or otherwise contained in this publication.

This publication is designed to provide accurate and authoritative information with regard to the subject matter covered herein. It is sold with the clear understanding that the Publisher is not engaged in rendering legal or any other professional services. If legal or any other expert assistance is required, the services of a competent person should be sought. FROM A DECLARATION OF PARTICIPANTS JOINTLY ADOPTED BY A COMMITTEE OF THE AMERICAN BAR ASSOCIATION AND A COMMITTEE OF PUBLISHERS.

Additional color graphics may be available in the e-book version of this book.

Library of Congress Cataloging-in-Publication Data

Names: Hansen, Amelia, 1964- editor.
Title: Privatization : policies, developments and challenges / editor, Amelia Hansen.
Other titles: Privatization (Nova Science Publishers)
Description: Hauppauge, New York : Nova Science Publishers, Inc., [2016] | Series: Business economics in a rapidly-changing world | Includes index.
Identifiers: LCCN 2016004809 (print) | LCCN 2016014052 (ebook) | ISBN 9781634847490 (hardcover) | ISBN 9781634847766 ()
Subjects: LCSH: Privatization.
Classification: LCC HD3850 .P7479 2016 (print) | LCC HD3850 (ebook) | DDC 338.9/25--dc23
LC record available at http://lccn.loc.gov/2016004809

Published by Nova Science Publishers, Inc. † New York

CONTENTS

PREFACE

Chapter One of *Privatization: Policies, Developments and Challenges* is to discuss the elements that caused the latest and current problems in the European economies and also, the imposed privatization (expropriation of the public wealth), as the remedy. This crisis started from the US and consequently, it was expanded to all economies of the world due to the systemic risk that globalization has induced to the developed and dependent nations. Thus, this European debt crisis is a crisis of capitalism. Chapter Two analyses different factors that may explain the changes in firms' performance after privatization in Europe. The final chapter explores how the American-based agro-industrial company Herakles Farm has thoroughly disregarded state and international laws and codes of conduct in the setting up of its contentious oil palm plantation that is largely located in-between protected areas in the ever-green forest of Southwest Cameroon.

In: Privatization
Editor: Amelia Hansen
ISBN: 978-1-63484-749-0
© 2016 Nova Science Publishers, Inc.

Chapter 1

The European Debt Crisis and the Imposed Privatization of the Public Wealth

John N. Kallianiotis*
Dr, Economics/Finance Department,
The Arthur J. Kania School of Management,
University of Scranton, Scranton, PA, US

Abstract

The purpose of this chapter is to discuss the elements that caused the latest and current problems in the European economies and also, the imposed privatization (expropriation of the public wealth), as the remedy. This crisis started from the US and consequently, it was expanded to all economies of the world, due to the systemic risk that globalization has induced to the developed and dependent nations. Thus, this European debt crisis is a crisis of capitalism. A recent historical retrospect is used to consider the evolution of events in the EU and the EMU before the crisis. The global uncertainty had increased the price of gold (decreased the value of the dollar, which increased artificially, the value of euro) and the debts and deficits had forced countries out of the financial market and with the help of speculators had heightened the interest rates. The

* John N. Kallianiotis, DR: Economics/Finance Department, The Arthur J. Kania School of Management, University of Scranton, Scranton, PA 18510-4602, tel: (570) 941-7577, fax: (570) 941-4825, e-mail: ioannis.kallianiotis@scranton.edu.

deregulation in financial markets and institutions, the easy money policy, and the subsidies by the EU had increased lending, corruption, speculation, prices in financial and real assets, and had caused an enormous bubble, which some people burst in 2008 and created the worst financial crisis, followed by the latest most severe recession in modern economic history. Also, the Greek debt crisis is emphasized together with the imposed privatization on Greek SOEs and on other European nations. A theoretical model of privatization and some political considerations to prevent crises and avoid expropriation of public wealth are discussed extensively.

INTRODUCTION

In this chapter, the elements that caused the recent and current problems in the European economies are discussed and also, how the EU tries to solve them by selling-off the indebted nations' public wealth ("privatization"). This unique crisis started from the capitalistic US and consequently, it was expanded to almost every economy of the world, due to the systemic risk that globalization has induced to the developed and controlled nations[1]. Thus, this crisis is a crisis of capitalism (a man-made inferior philosophical system). A historical retrospect is used to consider the evolution of events in the EU and the EMU before the crisis and during this prolonged crisis for eight years. The global uncertainty had increased the price of gold[2] (decreased the value of the dollar)[3] and the US debts and deficits had caused a depreciation of the dollar, which with the help of speculators had heightened the price of oil[4] until the Fall of 2014 and had created a commodity bubble. The deregulation in financial markets and institutions and the easy money policy by the Fed had

---

[1] The BRICS nations have not been affected, due to their negative correlation with the western economies and nations. We have two extreme philosophical economic systems in our world; capitalism and communism, which are against humanity and against sovereign nations and their citizens, wherever either one of them has been imposed, countries are in real trouble. Lately, the indicators show that capitalism is worse than communism. Of course, as humanists, we reject both of them.

[2] The price of gold from \$320.00/oz (2003:03) reached \$1,896.50/oz (2011:09). A growth of 492.656% in 8.5 years (57.96% per annum). On August 5, 2015, it was \$1,084.80/oz.

[3] See, Kallianiotis (2013b, 215-242).

[4] The price of oil from \$28.4/barrel (2003:05) reached \$144.15/barrel (2008:07); a growth of 412.26% in 5 years (82.45% per annum). On August 5, 2015, it was \$45.08/barrel (it is used as a weapon against the oil producers to affect negatively their economies in order to submit).

increased lending, corruption in business[5] and governments, speculation, prices in financial and real assets (even in food) and had caused an enormous bubble, which some people (the world planners)[6] burst in 2008 and created the worst financial crisis, followed by the latest most severe recession in modern economic history. The "enslaved" EU is copying the US and fell in the same trap, which caused the European economic crisis[7].

The moral, ethical, political, and financial crisis in the western free-market (actually, value-free) economies led them in deep recessions, enormous unemployment, annihilation of their wealth, complete distrust for the financial markets, a new cold war, an elevation of terrorism, and the millions of illegal immigrants and refugees[8] that the West's foreign policy generated in Middle East and North Africa. We will describe the sequence of events first and then the benefits (gains) and costs (losses) to the society by considering some basic action and policies (especially, the forced privatization), which might affect negatively the objective macroeconomic variables and cause an enormous loss of the public wealth for the countries. European nations and their people face an absolutely uncertain future because they have lost their national currencies, their central bank, their public policies, even their freedom of speech, their national educational systems, their objective history, their indigenous values, their traditions, their identity, and their sovereignty. Now, they are forced to sell-off their SOEs without their will. The powerless European governments are just inactively watching the events that we are all part and responsible (especially, the academic environment) for this irrational, interdependent, and complex world, which was designed and created for the control of the people.

In addition, it is presented a theoretical and graphical model and it is discussed the pros and cons of imposed privatizations (transferring the ownership and management of state-owned enterprises to private foreign firms) in Europe and especially in Greece and their effects on the economy,

---

[5] The recent emissions scandal of the German car manufacturer Volkswagen (VW) is one of the thousands of different cases of a deep business corruption in all industries, every day; these events are the most common in news. See, http://www.theguardian.com/business/live/2015/sep/24/volkswagen-scandal-vw-germany-counts-cost-of-crisis-after-ceo-quits-live-updates Also, http://www.telegraph.co.uk/finance/newsbysector/industry/11887711/VW-scandal-BMW-shares-plunge-after-SUV-breaches-EU-emissions-standards-live.html. The crisis might spill to the broader German economy because VW has deep ties to the German government (Lower Saxony owns 20% of VW). See, The Wall Street Journal, September 24, 2015, pp. A1 and A12.

[6] There are many experts' quotations that give a good inside of this latest planned financial crisis. You can request them from the author or from different websites.

[7] See, https://en.wikipedia.org/wiki/European_debt_crisis.

[8] See, http://www.nytimes.com/2015/09/22/opinion/roger-cohen-more-efficiency-less-humanity.html?_r = 0.

financial markets, employment, national wealth, and social welfare. Moderate privatizations, under normal conditions, might increase efficiency, productivity, liquidity in the financial markets, and their proceeds might reduce the national debts, if the country is not in financial distress and depression; but, at the same time, privatizations cause enormous unemployment, dependency on foreign capital and multinational firms, and the worst of all countries lose their national wealth, private monopolies are thriving, and the social welfare is declining. The European integration with its strange Maastricht criteria that only two countries were satisfying them (France and Luxemburg), the common overvalued euro for thirteen years, the recent debt crises and the austerity measures by the Troika [European Commission (Eurogroup), European Central Bank (ECB), and International Monetary Fund (IMF)] have created an enormous social cost to the member-nations (mainly in Greece) and the benefits from this non-democratic union are too small to cover its cost; especially, the loss of public policy for the members and the loss of national sovereignty are irreplaceable. The optimal level of privatization is the one that maximizes the social welfare (at the point, where the marginal benefits of privatization are equal to the marginal cost of socio-economic distress) and does not eliminate the wealth of the nation. The best remedy for the nations is to prevent crises and not to mend them because their social costs are colossal and affect human beings.

The literature on the European economic crisis is huge. All academics, politicians, and media are talking and trying to analyze this unique phenomenon in economic history and to explain the logic of the anti-growth policies that authorities are using and perpetuate the crisis. Stiglitz (2002) is criticizing the globalization due to the problems that is causing to the advanced economies. Kallianiotis (2007a) and (2007b) analyzes the factors that have caused the overvaluation of the euro and its negative effects on the Euro-zone member-nations. Bullard, Neely, and Wheelock (2009) discuss the financial crisis and the new systemic risk that has affected the global economic system. Wessel (2009) gives a very good chronological presentation of the global financial crisis. Kallianiotis (2013a and b) mentions that the common currency is worse than the fixed exchange rate for the countries that have adopted it. Rickards (2014) is talking about the future collapse of the international monetary system. Sposi and Grossman (2014) are referring to deindustrialization of the western nations and the redeployment of workers to low pay jobs. Williamson (2014) criticizes the new monetary policy that is pursued by the US Fed. Kallianiotis (2015d) says that the common public policy and the common currency in Euro-zone do not help the member-nations to improve their economies and overcome the recession.

Also, the literature on privatization that has been imposed by some (neo-liberal entities, like the Troika), who believe that it might increase efficiency of the public sector, but it contributes further to the weakening of the public sector; since public assets are sold at very low prices that are not even compensated for the loss of future revenue from these public companies. Actually, these forced privatizations are expropriations of the national wealth, which is against the social welfare of the citizens. Studies by Kay and Thompson (1986) and Wortzel and Wortzel (1989) suggested that privatizations did not promote economic efficiency, only governments have raised significant revenues through the sale of SOEs. Sappington and Stiglitz (1987) addressed issues related to state versus private ownership and they favored state ownership, together with many other studies. Bhaskar and Khan (1995) in a study of the Jute industry in Bangladesh found that privatization had a large and significant negative effect on the employment of white-collar workers, while the reduction in output is not statistically significant. Parker (1999) reviews privatization in each of the member states of the EU; he identifies the differences in the levels of privatization activity, and explains that privatization may not lead to efficiency, but to redistribution of income and economic power. Morgen (2001) says that devolution and privatization have marked the neoliberal agenda of downsizing the state and minimizing its role in regulating and ameliorating the operation of the market[9]. Alexiou (2003, 26) says that, "the contractionary nature of the policies imposed upon the EU member states, to arguably facilitate their transition into the monetary union appear to, at least in the short run, have created an economic environment that is far from conducive to employment creation. Lack of strategies that target real, rather than nominal variables, permeates current economic policy as this is run by the think-tanks of an independent European Central Bank and its affiliated institutions." Becker (2007) deals with privatization of water and waste public firms in EU and he does not expect full privatization of these monopolistic companies. Luechinger, Meier, and Stutzer (2008) say that high general unemployment reduces individual welfare even

[9] "Devolution is the transfer or decentralization of government functions from higher to lower of the federal hierarchy. Privatization is the shift of state services, assets or functions to nonstate sectors, especially the market, which is further implicated in shrinking the state. It also represents a reordering of claims in a society, as a general movement of institutional design, privatization undermines the foundation of claims for public purpose and public service." See, Morgen (2001, 747).

for people, who are still employed and the public sector attracts more risk-averse individuals than does the private sector. Kallianiotis (2009) warns that vast privatizations have caused huge social welfare losses. Kallianiotis and Dragone (2009) said that privatization in EU has become the only trend the last years, even though that has been economically and political disruptive. Kallianiotis (2011c) shows that privatization beyond an optimal level makes social welfare negative. Kallianiotis (2012) deals with the latest imposed privatizations on the high debt nations, like Greece. Kallianiotis (2013c) refers to the optimal level of privatization as the one that its marginal benefits are equal to the marginal cost of socio-economic distress. Then, excess privatization causes serious social welfare problems to our societies and politicians must avoid it, even though that international institutions try to inflict this "New Age" policy on poor nations.

Recent Historical Retrospect of the European Crises

Europeans have gone a long way for thousands of years and had reached a high point of social development, morality, ethics, philosophy, democracy, civilization, and even were waiting for the "True God," due to the Greek contribution[10], who came five centuries later from the golden century of Athens. Then, with the revealed Truth new hope appeared for the people, especially in the Eastern Roman (Byzantine, Medieval Greek) Empire and the entire Europe, the "Christendom." Consequently, the development in Europe was enormous after the adoption of the ancient Greek moral philosophy, civilization, Christianity, and reaching its industrial revolution; but, behind every good effort there are other (dark) powers with suspicious objectives. One of these objectives, the top one, is globalization (global control of all the nations), which started with the integration of the European nations; but, it requires elimination of the national governments, which can be done by generating crises and then, by taking away their public wealth (privatization). This long planned process is succeeding (artificially) with the European Union, so there will be no objections and oppositions from any other developing or underdeveloped nation. Of course, the plan is the opponents to

[10] See, Kallianiotis (2014b).

be crashed to prevent "contagion" to other nations, as it happened with the Greek referendum on July 5, 2015[11].

The EEC started on January 1, 1958 (with the Treaty of Rome signed on March 25, 1957) and continued with the EU in 1993[12], with the EMU in 1999, its central bank (ECB, in Frankfurt, Germany) in 1998, its institutions[13], its regulations[14] and directives[15], its constitution[16] (Treaty of Lisbon) without

[11] The Greek leftish party SYRIZA, which had won the elections on January 25, 2015, asked the citizens to have a referendum, if they want a third memorandum and 62% of them voted NO. Unfortunately, the EU does not consider these democratic solutions because it does not believe so much in democracy, as its history shows.

[12] The Maastricht Treaty established the European Union under its current name in 1993 and introduced European citizenship. The latest major amendment to the constitutional basis (that took out the Christian foundations of Europe), which was renamed as the Treaty of Lisbon, came into force in 2009. The EU has developed a single market through a standardized system of laws that apply in all member states. There are 28 member-nations (they call them "states") with 24 official languages, and a population of 506,913,394 people and a GDP of $18.495 trillion and per capita income of $36,479 (in 2014). Within the Schengen Area, passport controls have been abolished (unfenced vineyard). EU policies aim to ensure the free movement of people, goods, services, and capital, enact legislation in "justice" and home affairs, and maintain common policies on trade, agriculture, fisheries, and regional development. The monetary union was established in 1999 and came into full force (was imposed by ignoring their own criteria) in 2002. It is currently composed of 19 member-states (they are not "nations" anymore because they have lost their sovereignty) that use the euro as their legal tender and there are 9 other currencies in the EU member-nations. Through the Common Foreign and Security Policy, the EU has developed a role in external relations and defense; but, all its member-nations are compulsory members of NATO (*sic*). The union maintains permanent diplomatic missions throughout the world and represents itself at the United Nations, the WTO, the G8, and the G-20 (lately, they left out Russia from these groups, due to the crisis that EU created in Ukraine by wanted to detach it from Russia and making it as a new member controlled by the EU). With a combined population of over 500 million inhabitants, or 7.3% of the world population, the EU in 2014 generated a nominal gross domestic product (GDP) of $18.495 trillion, constituting approximately 24% of global nominal GDP and 17% when measured in terms of purchasing power parity. As of 2014, the EU has the largest economy in the world, generating a GDP bigger than any other economic union or country (The same year 2014, the US had a real GDP of $16.295 trillion and China $16.480 trillion). See, http://knoema.com/nwnfkne/world-gdp-ranking-2015-data-and-charts.

[13] The institutions of the European Union are the seven (7) principal decision making bodies of the European Union. They are, as listed in Article 13 of the Treaty on European Union: (1) the European Parliament, (2) the European Council, (3) the Council of the European Union, (4) the European Commission, (5) the Court of Justice of the European Union, (6) the European Central Bank and (7) the Court of Auditors. Institutions are different from agencies of the European Union.

[14] A regulation is a legal act of the European Union that becomes immediately enforceable as law in all member-states simultaneously. Regulations can be distinguished from directives which, at least in principle, need to be transposed into national law. Regulations can be adopted by means of a variety of legislative procedures depending on their subject matter.

[15] A directive is a legal act of the European Union, which requires member states to achieve a particular result without dictating the means of achieving that result. It can be distinguished

referenda in 2009, which was imposed undemocratically to poor Europeans with pressure on the controlled politicians of the 28 member-nations (they call them "states")[17]. The fixed exchange rate was abandoned in March 1973 because it did not work and the EU chose something worse than the fixed exchange rate, the common currency in 2002 (the euro, €) for its completely different nations that was imposed forcefully (without the nations satisfying the Maastricht criteria)[18] to 19 so far poor nations and their citizens, which caused the loss of competitiveness of these economies and they have to do "internal devaluations" to compete with the rest of the world. What a deceit, treason, and criminal decision by the Brussels and the politicians of the member-nations! The Euro-zone nations are and will be in trouble in the future, too, because they lost their central bank, their domestic currency, their public policies, their independence, their sovereignty, and their indigenous

from regulations which are self-executing and do not require any implementing measures. Directives normally leave member-states with a certain amount of leeway as to the exact rules to be adopted. Directives can be adopted by means of a variety of legislative procedures depending on their subject matter.

[16] The European Constitution was turned down in the member-nations that had referenda. This Treaty was signed on October 29, 2004 by representatives of the then 25 member-nations. It was later ratified by 18 member states, which included referendums endorsing it in Spain and Luxembourg. However the rejection of the document by French and Dutch voters in May and June 2005 brought the ratification process to an end and changed the name of the Constitution to the Treaty of Lisbon. After the French and Dutch referendum results, European leaders decided to hold a "period of reflection" on what to do next. As part of this reflection period a "group of wise men" was set up to consider possible courses of action. This group, known as the Amato Group, of high-level European politicians – former prime ministers, ministers and members of the European Commission – first met on September 30, 2006 in Rome. In the June 2007 European summit meeting, member-nations "agreed" to abandon the constitution and to amend the existing treaties, which would remain in force. The new treaty, which had previously been referred to as the *Reform Treaty*, became the Lisbon Treaty because it was signed in Lisbon on December 13, 2007 and was ratified by the EU parliaments, without any referenda. Another indication of the "democratic" (actually, dictatorial) procedures in EU.

[17] https://en.wikipedia.org/wiki/Member_state_of_the_European_Union.

[18] The Greek prime minister at the time, a Semite (from the tribe of Shem, a son of Noah), Costas Semites paid €400 million to Goldman Sachs to manipulate the public accounts for Greece to enter the Euro-zone. See, http://www.spiegel.de/international/europe/greek-debt-crisis-how-goldman-sachs-helped-greece-to-mask-its-true-debt-a-676634.html. See also, http://www.nytimes.com/2010/02/14/business/global/14debt.html?pagewanted=all&_r=0. Costas Semites' government was the one that destroyed the Hellenic-Orthodox traditional culture in Greece with their suspicious "modernization" (ἐκσυγχρονισταί). See, http://www.antibaro.gr/article/13596. The question is, now; how these people, the main contributors to the current Greek crisis, who destroyed Greece and made the proud and historic Greek people a global mockery are still out of the jail?

culture, values, and freedom. These nations became colonies of Brussels (actually, German protectorates)[19].

Globalization generated a new global risk (the systemic risk), due to the high positive correlations that has caused among the world economies (except the BRICS). After the US financial crisis, the European debt crisis (often also referred to as the Eurozone crisis or the European sovereign debt crisis) started, which is a multi-year debt crisis that has been taking place in the EU since the end of 2009. Several Euro-zone member-nations (Greece, Portugal, Ireland, Spain, and Cyprus) were unable to repay or refinance (rollover the old debt with new one, as all the other nations are doing) their government debt or to bail out their over-indebted banks under their national supervision (because they have lost their central banks and their national currencies, they cannot monetize their national debts) without the assistance of third parties, like other Euro-zone countries (European Commission), the ECB or the IMF (the infamous Troika).

Of course, if a nation is not independent, self-sufficient, free, democratic, and negotiates with its partners by compromising its values and paideia, soon it will be in crisis and the crisis had started with its accession to EU, which appeared as an economic crisis in 2008 that was developed in the US, another union of 50 states, which is also in trouble, as the 28 states in EU[20]. But, the US dollar, at the moment, as an international reserve currency and the Fed supplying these greenbacks (Fed's liabilities backed by government debt) in trillions to finance the government and private debts, the country was "saved" with an unemployment over 23%[21] and a recession that is still going on[22]. The

[19] Greece is under German control since 1832, when a German, Otto, became the first King of Greece after her partial liberation from the Ottoman yoke. See, Protopresvyteros George Metallinos (1992) and Kallianiotis (2015c).

[20] The EU is in a recession for many years; the growth of the GDP was:

	2005	2006	2007	2008	2009	2010	2011	2012
EU-28:	2.0%	3.4%	3.1%	0.5%	- 4.4%	2.1%	1.7%	-0.4%
EU-19:	1.7%	3.2%	3.0%	0.5%	- 4.5%	2.0%	1.6%	-0.7%

	2013	2014	2005-2014.
EU-28:	0.0%	1.3%	9.3%.
EU-19:	-0.5%	0.9%	7.2%.

See also, http://data.worldbank.org/indicator/NY.GDP.MKTP.KD.ZG/countries/EU?display=graph. In addition, see, https://en.wikipedia.org/wiki/Economy_of_the_European_Union And the unemployment rate from 5.3% (Germany) to 27.3% (Greece).

[21] Official unemployment in the US reached 10.2% (2009:10), but independent studies measure it to be more than double from the government statistics. See, http://www.shadowstats.com/alternate_data/unemployment-charts.

[22] The US real GDP growth cannot recover since 2008. It was, 2008Q01: - 2.7017%, 2008Q02: 2.0001%, 2008Q03: - 1.9056%, 2008Q04: - 8.1864%, 2009Q01: - 5.4288%, 2009Q02: - 0.5387%, 2009Q03: 1.3132%, 2009Q04: 3.9281%, 2010Q01: 1.7414%, 2010Q02:

financial market collapsed in the US and this contagion effect was spread to all the financial markets in EU member-nations. The peak of this stock market bubble was on October 9, 2007 (DJIA was 14,164.53) and its trough on March 9, 2009 (DJIA was 6,547.05), a decline of - 7,617.48 points or by the percentage of -53.78%, and with calendar days to bottom 517[23]. Investors "lost" $18 trillion from their wealth; actually, it was distributed from the naïve investors to the hawk speculators. This is today's unregulated stock market; a casino that can destroy the entire real economy[24].

The US economy had long been characterized by international imbalances in its current and capital accounts and enormous public and private debts[25] that

3.9208%, 2010Q03: 2.7293%, 2010Q04: 2.5432%, 2011Q01: - 1.5360%, 2011Q02: 2.9430%, 2011Q03: 0.8432%, 2011Q04: 4.5824%, 2012Q01: 2.2491%, 2012Q02: 1.6255%, 2012Q 03: 2.4902%, 2012Q04: 0.0622%, 2013Q01: 2.7413%, 2013Q02: 1.7672%, 2013Q03: 4.5162%, 2013Q04: 3.5001%, 2014Q01: - 2.1068%, 2014Q02: 4.5920%, 2014Q03: 4.9667%, 2014Q04: 2.2174%, 2015Q01: 0.6430%, 2015Q02: 2.3219%, and 2015Q03: 1.49%. See, http://sub1.economagic.com/em-cgi/data.exe/var/rgdp -qtrchg.

[23] The DJIA plunged on September 29, 2008 by 777.68 points or 7%, as fears grew that more banks could fail, because the House sent the Bush administration's $700 billion rescue package to defeat (*The Wall Street Journal*, September 30, 2008, pp. A1, A3, C1, and C8). The DJIA fell by 13% in five days in October 2008 (*The Wall Street Journal*, October 8, 2008, p. C1). Also, see, *Yahoo/Finance*, October 13, 2008 and *Bloomberg.com*, November 20, 2008. On February 19, 2009, the DJIA fell by - 89.68 to its lowest value. (*Bloomberg.com*, 2/19/2009 and *The Wall Street Journal*, February 24, 2009, pp. A1 and C1). Stocks hit April 1997 level, signaling long slump, the DJIA lost 299.64 points (-4.24%) in a single day. The same happened to all markets around the world (due to globalization) on this disastrous Monday (March 2, 2009): Hong Kong (Hang Seng) - 3.9%; India (Bombay Sensex) - 3.2%; Japan (Nikkei) - 3.8%; France (CAC 40) - 4.5%; Germany (DAX) - 3.5%; UK (FTSE) - 5.3%; Brazil (Bovespa) - 5.1%; Canada (S&P/TSX) - 5.4% (*The Wall Street Journal*, March 3, 2009, pp. A1, A4, C1, and C2). The DJIA fell another 37.27 points (- 0.6%) and investors hope that this is the bottom (*The Wall Street Journal*, March 4, 2009, pp. A1 and C1). The DJIA fell - 281.40 points on March 5, 2009 (*Bloomberg.com*, March 5 and 9, 2009). The DJIA took just 17 months to plunge from its 2007 high to its 2009 low. But it took four years to recoup its losses and reach its previous level of 14,253.77 on Tuesday, March 5, 2013 (*The Wall Street Journal*, March 5, 2013, pp. A1, A8, A9, and C1). But, a new bubble was constructed in the financial market, due to quantitative easing by the Fed; the DJIA reached 18,312.39 on May 19, 2015 (a growth of 11,765.34 points or 179.70% in 6 years; 29.95% growth per annum). Lately (October 14, 2015), it was 16,917.00; the bubble has started losing air.

[24] See, https://en.wikipedia.org/wiki/Sovereign_default.

[25] Total US debt (public and private) was: $186.061 trillion (2015Q1), which is 1,141.85% of the GDP. And the world is talking only about the Greek debt, which was (in 2014): €317.1 billion, with a GDP of €179.1 billion; then, the national debt was 177.1% of the GDP, with an annual interest payment on this debt of €22.3 billion. The private debt was €251.6 billion. Thus, total debt (public and private) was: €568.7 billion (317.53% of the GDP). See, https://en.wikipedia.org/wiki/Greek_government-debt_crisis and http://moneymorning.com/2015/03/25/how-much-does-greece-owe-4-charts-that-put-greek-debt-in-perspective/ Also, https://www.cia.gov/library/publications/the-world-factbook/fields/2079.html.

have to be financed heavily by foreign capital and by money printing (Fed's reserves). The quantitative easing of the Fed is something that we see for the first time in Economic history[26]. The monetary base from $874.826 billion (9/10/2008) reached $4,139.322 billion (1/21/2015)[27]. Last year, the Fed signaled that it would keep rates near zero until the midyear 2015[28]; but, they continue to postpone an increase in federal funds rate because there is no improvement in the economy[29]. At the same time the US and many EU countries lost their agriculture and manufacturing and became pure service economies that are very vulnerable to business cycles and have experienced enormous unemployment1[30], reduction in income, and destruction of the small cities, towns, and country sides of their nations. Some strange (globalists) economists believe that these ruins of the domestic main sectors of the economies (agricultural and industrial) are normal and they call these detrimental processes as "structural transformations"[31]. These policies are exactly what some ignorant politicians (betrayers) imposed on Greece and made the country dependent on Germans. The ECB did not increase the monetary base, which has contributed to the deep recessions. It was €899.514

---

[26] Smithers, founder of Smithers and Co. in London, said in a phone interview to Bloomberg: "QE is a very dangerous policy, in my view, because it has pushed asset prices up and high asset prices, we know from history, are very dangerous. It is very strongly indicated by reliable measures that we're looking at a stock market which is something like 80 percent over-priced." See, http://www.bloomberg.com/news/articles/2015-05-18/nobel-winner-s-math-shows-s-p-500-unhinged-from-reality-or-not. See also, http://www.levyinstitute.org/pubs/op_49.pdf.

[27] A growth of 373.16% in 6.5 years (57.41% p.a.). See, FRED, Federal Reserve Bank of St. Luis. Also, see, Williamson (2014). Lately (9/16/2015), the monetary base increased further to $4,165.401 billion. See, https://research.stlouisfed.org/fred2/series/BASE/.

[28] See, *The Wall Street Journal*, January 29, 2015, pp. A1 and A2.

[29] The FOMC decided on September 17, 2015 to continue with this zero federal funds rate until next year. See, http://www.theguardian.com/business/live/2015/sep/17/us-federal-reserve-interest-rate-decision-markets-janet-yellen-live. Also, http://www.bloomberg.com/news/articles/2015-09-22/yellen-speech-a-chance-for-her-to-confirm-or-deny-2015-liftoff. On December 15, 2015, the Fed raised the target rate to 0.50%. See, http://www.wsj.com/articles/fed-raises-rates-after-seven-years-at-zero-expects-gradual-tightening-path-1450292616?mg=id-wsj.

[30] "Tackling the Real Unemployment Rate: 12.6%." See, http://www.forbes.com/sites/louisefron/2014/08/20/tackling-the-real-unemployment-rate-12-6/. Also, other sources give an unemployment of 23% in October 2014 and in January 2015, it was 23.2%. See, http://www.shadowstats.com/alternate_data/unemployment-charts. European unemployment was: The Euro area seasonally-adjusted unemployment rate was 10.9% in July 2015, down from 11.6% in July 2014. The EU-28 unemployment rate was 9.5% in July 2015; with Germany's 4.7% and Greece' unemployment 25.0%. See, http://ec.europa.eu/eurostat/statistics-explained/index.php/Unemployment_statistics.

[31] See, Sposi and Grossman (2014).

billion (September 2008) and became €1,292.102 billion (January 2015)[32]. These current European crises proved that countries must have their own central bank, their own national currency, and their own public policies, otherwise, these crises will become permanent.

In October 2008, a bailout package became necessary to be offered by the EU governments to restore confidence in their economies. But the deregulated and corrupted banks had made too many bad loans, which have created big holes in their balance sheets. Financial ministers were buying up the bad assets and putting the risk onto European taxpayers, hoping that banks would use this money to restart lending, but some of this money was paid as dividends to their shareholders and bonuses to their executives. The taxpayers are the losers in our corrupted financial system and its institutions. The Euro-zone economies had been sustained by excessive borrowing for many years (with a total, EU 28, governments debts) as of September 24, 2015 of over €12.411 trillion, €24,641 per capita, 89.153% of its total GNP, which was in 2014, €13.921 trillion[33]. Also, unemployment was increasing and personal income and consumption were falling. Exports were declining and the tax revenues for the governments were diminishing. The confidence level of consumers and investors had reached the lowest level since the introduction of these indexes. All these contingencies were negatively affecting the financial sector of the economy, which is the only sector left to sustain production, growth, and employment for these service oriented economies. The number of jobs lost in EU28 were 25.91 million in 2013. Greece lost 1.364 million jobs, which became the biggest humanitarian crisis for the country. The worst crisis for a person is to be unemployed, for this reason there were thousands of suicides[34]. The objective of the governments, central banks[35], and the other authorities

[32] A growth of 43.64% in 6.5 years (6.71% p.a.). This monetary policy is completely unacceptable in the middle of a depression in EMU. See, http://sdw.ecb.europa.eu/quickview.do?SERIES_KEY = 123.ILM.M.U2.C.LT01.Z5.EUR.

[33] The EU is in real trouble with these tremendous debts, which are unsustainable for some nations and its future is very uncertain and due to globalization, the world's future is questionable. Dark powers will take advantage of this negative real savings and will cause serious financial crises in the near future, so that they can pursue their ultimate objective, the global slavery. Except, if it would be a reaction by the voters of the countries, as it happened in Greece during the elections of January 25, 2015, where they voted against the Troika's austerities and its globalization that led the country to its worst humanitarian catastrophe in its 7,000 years old history. See, http://www.eudebtclock.org/.

[34] Of course, a suicide is the worst crime for the Orthodox Christian and it is not allowed. People have to endure with hope every difficulties in their life. The belief in God is the only remedy. But, Europeans were forced to abandon God with their "modernizations."

[35] The evidence have shown to everyone that the philosophical systems (capitalism = the sub-culture of waste and communism = the sub-culture of oppression), which this (the same)

must be to prevent crises and maximize their nations' social welfare, but these controlled policy makers and regulators have no power and consequently, have lost control of the market and of the entire socio-political-economic system.

The "irrational exuberance" that Euro-subsidies and low interest rate loans gave to Europeans, is over after three decades of wastefulness, greediness, briberies, frauds, lies, and corruption. But this was expected because the EU economies and their markets were too good to be true[36]. They were living a big delusion and this deceit is over. The economic and social indicators reveal that even the US from a moral, ethical, and just superpower is becoming less and less competitive[37] and less friendly with the rest of the world[38]. The European Union (the forced integration of 28 nations, without referenda), with its debt crises, and 19 of them with a common currency (common central bank)[39] has proved to be the worst "innovation" in human history. It is a mixture of twenty eight nations without domestic public policies, without self-determination, without sovereignty, and of course, without any future[40]. All these strange evolutions have increased the global uncertainty, have caused

group of people have imposed on societies for more than three centuries do not work, but satisfy their false needs for global hegemony and universal slavery. Of course, we (who know the truth) will say NO to them! Some nations have started their opposition to this global servitude.

[36] This was the cost of being "European." Ὁ ἐξευρωπαϊσμός, ὁ ὁποῖος ἀποτελεῖ τήν πνευματικήν πανούκλαν, κατά τόν Φώτη Κόντογλου.

[37] Extreme capitalism does not work because it is against people's interest.

[38] The US was the biggest economic power in the world and is declining daily because of its control by the market. Greece was the biggest spiritual power on earth and is descending daily, due to its corrupted and controlled politicians, who did not believe in the Hellenic-Orthodox values. We must grieve for the plight of these two nations and some people are responsible for this. The problem must be the bad and controlled leadership (New Age followers) in these two "model" nations.

[39] The ECB occupies a gleaming thirty-seven-story skyscraper in Frankfurt's financial district and its objective is to avoid another intra-European war and to rival the United States. Both the Fed and ECB were structured as political compromises. The Fed has only one set of elected politicians to cope with; the ECB has at the moment nineteen (19 EMU member-nations). The legal mandate is for the first to maximize employment and price stability; for the second is to resist inflation. Both central banks are designed to be independent, but they are not; they depend on the market and financial institutions. Both concentrate on the same intermediate objectives: credit and liquidity. The central banks can create money ("printing money," which is electronic) to satisfy the ultimate objective of the nations, their social welfare, but so far both have been ineffective.

[40] For example, in EU, 73.8% are against privatization, 80.9% are against Turkey's entrance to EU, 83.6% are against Euro-constitution (Treaty of Lisbon), 71.6% want to go back to their previous national currencies, 71.5% of Greeks are in favor of vetoing Skopje's (Vardarska's) entrance to NATO and EU, Europeans are against the independence of Kosovo, and 86.1% of Greeks are against the marriage of homosexuals (*e-grammes.gr*, different polls). Prudent Europeans are actually against this "anti-European creature," the EU.

unemployment in EU[41], have reduced competitiveness, and have augmented poverty, anxiety, and health problems (mental[42] and physical) to their citizens.

The free-market system with its new innovation, the globalization through integration of the nations, has failed and needs more government regulation; more independence and self-determination for the nations, and better corporate governance for the MNCs that led domestic firms to bankruptcy and people to permanent unemployment (misery). Governments had to bailout a corrupted financial system, even when the deficits and the national debts are astronomical[43]. But, they had no other option, except to "rob responsible Americans [and Europeans] and pay the robbers of the financial market"[44]. Then, what are the social benefits? Why we need these global changes and "evolutions," which are against humanity? Why we want to take away the public wealth from the nations' citizens? Why are we acting anti-socially and against people's interest? The latest financial crisis (with a combination of large failures, costly bailouts, deep recessions, and destruction of entire countries) might be able to change the perception of the social welfare effects of the thirty years of deregulation and the fifty years of European integration. The Fed was instructed by Congress in 1977 to aim at "maximum employment" and "stable prices," but it cares for price stability (Bernanke considered inflation target)[45]. The ECB does not have employment as its mandate. Even though, Europeans have to continue to fight and hope that they will gain their national sovereignty soon.

But, many questions remain, even today, for the abandoned Europeans. Who are to blame for the latest debt crises, the peculiar recessions that they caused, and the continuation of the humanitarian crises? The responsible parties must be the followings:

---

[41] The main reasons for unemployment in Europe are the illegal and uncontrolled immigration and the austerities in the middle of depression. Europe is in trouble to lose its thousands years old identity.

[42] Gunmen opened fire in lecture halls at universities or in offices killing or injuring people before they been killed or commit suicide. These incidents are very often in the US; lately, Europeans started mimicking US, too. We tried to abandon God and level down the indigenous traditional values from the nations.

[43] For Europe, the budget deficits and national debts (in 2011) were; EU28: 4.5% and 83%, Eurozone17: 4.1% and 88%, Hungary: - 4.3% (surplus) and 80.6%, Estonia: - 1% (surplus) and 6%, Ireland: 13% and 108.2%, and Greece: 9.1% and 165.3%.

[44] Dr. Shannon Grimes in *Tahlequah Daily Press*, September 25, 2008.

[45] The ECB, the Bank of England, and the Bank of Japan have only one explicit goal: price stability. See, Wessel (2009, 86). Fed's policy is ineffective during the latest financial crisis. See also, http://www.nakedcapitalism.com/2014/10/matt-stoller-why-is-alan-greenspans-lawyer-scott-alvarez-still-controlling-the-federal-reserve-aig-bailout-trial.html.

1. European politicians, who joined the Euro-zone without a referendum.
2. Corrupted governments and institutions, which acted against social interest.
3. Countries, who consume beyond their production and generated these debts and deficits.
4. The EU households, who have spent way beyond their means in recent years; they have to start saving, as their fathers did (it was shame a person to have a debt).
5. The unregulated banks, who took the upside and left the downside to the taxpayers.
6. The involvement of the neo-liberal IMF in Euro-zone debt crisis and bailouts.
7. The ECB's low liquidity and capital controls towards the member-nations.
8. The European integration that imposes the same policy on completely different nations.
9. The German anti-growth austerity policies in periods of recession.
10. The EMU that restricted the public policy and sovereignty of the member-nations.
11. The globalization and the pseudo-leaders, who follow this New Age inhumane servitude.
12. The expropriation of the national wealth from the indebted nations.

The right wealth must be created through saving, ingenuity, entrepreneurship, hard work, a fair tax system, ethical business procedures, investment in human capital, and moderation in spending (waste). Of course, many try to create wealth by extracting wealth from others through inflation, price discrimination, overpricing their products and services, due to inelastic demands, inside information, and market manipulation. This is not wealth creation, but wealth redistribution from the naïve citizens to the greedy and shrewd opportunists. For these reasons, markets have to be regulated and the system to be restructured. The global financial system is so complex that with each financial collapse the systemic risk is growing exponentially. The global system with all these derivatives ($691 trillion with June 2014)[46], which are a

[46] Some of the more common derivatives include forwards, futures, options, swaps, and variations of these such as collateralized debt obligations, credit default swaps, and mortgage-backed securities. Most derivatives are traded over-the-counter (off-exchange) or on an exchange such as the Chicago Mercantile Exchange, while most insurance contracts have developed into a separate industry. See, http://www.bis.org/statistics/derstats.htm.

surprise to bankers and regulators, is on the knife-edge of collapse. If a catastrophe unfolds, it is too late to stop. Crises have to be prevented through regulations. It is a pity for the Euro-zone member-nations to have lost their sovereignty and become protectorates of Brussels (Germany)[47] and they cannot govern their own country. The first priority of any sovereign, democratic, value oriented, and advanced nation is the welfare of its citizens and neither to satisfy the demands of the corrupted and inhumane markets and their institutions and nor those of the EU and the lenders (that must know the risk of lending). The world is enslaved by the corrupted markets and this cannot continue because our well-being is in trouble.

THE GREEK DEBT CRISIS

The Greek government-debt crisis (actually, the Greek "planned" depression and occupation)[48] started in late 2009. It was the first of five sovereign debt crises (Portugal, Ireland, Italy, Greece, and Spain)[49] in the Euro-zone (the 19 nations that have lost their central banks, their national currencies, and their public policies); later, Cyprus was added and it referred to collectively, as the European debt crisis. In Greece, triggers included the turmoil of a great recession[50], structural weaknesses in the Greek economy (a political crisis), and a sudden crisis in confidence among lenders (Greek government securities had difficulties to be accepted by the market). In late 2009, fears developed about Greece's ability to meet its debt obligations, due

---

[47] Germany is a very dangerous nation as history can prove it and it has to be isolated from the rest of Europe for its crimes against humanity during the 20th and the 21st centuries and for the past one thousand years (since the crusades 1095-1291). See, http://www.crimesofwar.org/a-z-guide/crimes-against-humanity/. Also, http://money.cnn.com/2015/05/14/news/greece-germany-war-video/.

[48] Today (October 28, 2015), that I am writing this section, Greece has the 75th anniversary of her OXI (NO) that Prime Minister Ioannis Metaxas said to the Axis (Italy and Germany) that wanted to pass through (occupy) Greece and they declared war (WWII) against this peaceful country (October 28, 1940). As we see, nothing has changed; these pseudo-"allies and partners" in EU continue with the same anti-Greek policy. Greece has to say the new OXI (NO) to all of them. See, *Christian Vivliografia*, October 27, 2015 for a big number of articles on this subject. https://christianvivliografia.wordpress.com/2015/10/27/%e1%bd%91%cf%80%ce%b5%cf%8d%ce%b8%cf%85%ce%bd%ce%b7-%cf%83%cf%85%ce%bd%ce%bf%ce%bb%ce%b9%ce%ba%e1%bd%b0-%e1%bc%a1-%ce%b3%ce%b5%cf%81%ce%bc%ce%b1%ce%bd%ce%b9%ce%ba%e1%bd%b4/.

[49] The unethical and insolent markets called them the PIIGS (χοίρους); others called them the GIPSI (ζητιάνους) nations.

[50] See, https://en.wikipedia.org/wiki/Greek_government-debt_crisis.

to revelations that previous data on government debt levels and deficits had been misreported by the Greek government. This led to a crisis of confidence, indicated by a widening of bond yield spreads and the cost of risk insurance on credit default swaps (CDSs)[51] compared to the other Euro-zone nations (Germany in particular). Germany wanted to experiment the effects of austerity on the Greek people and it destroyed this historic nation[52]. In 2012, Greece's government was close to default and the nation had the largest (the country had defaulted 5 times in the past) sovereign debt default in its history[53]. On June 30, 2015, Greece became the first developed nation that failed (or it was her reaction to the Troika's inhumane pressure) to make an IMF loan repayment. At that time, Greece's government had debts of €323 billion[54]. This loan to IMF was paid a little later. But, there is currently no proposed solution for the Greek crisis that does not involve substantial pain for one or more constituencies[55].

The conflicting forces of our time are enormous and for small nations, like Greece, which is based on a traditional value system, it is very difficult to resist to the outside anti-democratic, neo-liberal, and New Age pressures.

---

[51] A credit default swap (CDS) is a financial swap agreement that the seller of the CDS will compensate the buyer (usually the creditor of the reference loan) in the event of a loan default (by the debtor) or other credit event. The seller of the CDS insures the buyer against some reference loan defaulting. The buyer of the CDS makes a series of payments (the CDS "fee" or "spread") to the seller and, in exchange, receives a payoff if the loan defaults. It was an "innovation" of JP Morgan in 1994. In the event of default the buyer of the CDS receives compensation (usually the FV of the loan), and the seller of the CDS takes possession of the defaulted loan. However, anyone can purchase a CDS, even buyers who do not hold the loan instrument and who have no direct insurable interest in the loan (these are called "naked" CDSs). If there are more CDS contracts outstanding than bonds in existence, a protocol exists to hold a credit event auction; the payment received is usually substantially less than the face value of the loan. Credit default swaps have existed since 1994, and increased in use after 2003. By the end of 2007, the outstanding CDS amount was $62.2 trillion, falling to $26.3 trillion by mid-year 2010 and reportedly $25.5 trillion in early 2012. CDSs are not traded on an exchange and there is no required reporting of transactions to a government agency. During the 2007-2010 financial crisis the lack of transparency in this large market became a concern to regulators as it could pose a huge systemic risk. In March 2010, the [DTCC] Trade Information Warehouse announced it would give regulators greater access to its credit default swaps database. See, "Media Statement: DTCC Policy for Releasing CDS Data to Global Regulators." Depository Trust and Clearing Corporation. March 23, 2010.

[52] See, http://www.levyinstitute.org/publications/the-greek-economic-crisis-and-the-experience-of-austerity.

[53] They were in 1826, 1843, 1860, 1893, and in 1932. See, http://www.ekathimerini.com/132726/article/ekathimerini/comment/a-greek-odyssey-1821-2201.

[54] See, https://en.wikipedia.org/wiki/Greek_government-debt_crisis.

[55] See, http://www.truth-out.org/opinion/item/32519-an-unexplored-side-of-the-greek-financial-crisis-two-economies-one-currency.

These collisions are: East versus West, country versus EU, nations versus markets, peoples' dignity versus complete indifference, truth versus lie, citizens versus allies, nation versus the world, spiritual world versus secular world, knowledge versus ignorance, patriotism versus globalism, individuals versus businesses, justice versus injustice, wealthy versus poor, democracy versus tyranny, liberty versus slavery, values versus distain, respect of life versus refusal of life, respect versus disrespect, liberalism versus conservatism, capitalism versus socialism, agreement versus abruption, integration versus independence, and many other conflicts. But, the objective of any knowledgeable society (nation), today, must be the welfare of the country and the perfection of its people, all the other goals are inferior and worthless. Orthodox Greeks have to say NO to all these external (foreign) delusions[56].

The latest debt crisis had its origin at the corruption in governments and businesses, which affected the financial and the housing markets. And this anticipated financial crisis because of the European integration, together with the high debts and prices of energy and food (due to lack of production and dependency on imports[57], lack of national currency and monetary policy) brought the economy to a deep recession. The failure of the unregulated large banks increased the systematic (market) risk and harmed other small firms and finally, the real sector of the economy and due to high positive correlation with the world economies from the globalization, the global (systemic)[58] risk became domestic. Another important type of risk to the Euro-zone member-nations is the lack of public policy, lack of national currency to exercise trade policy, lack of public central bank to absorb the national debt and provide the liquidity to the banks, the capital controls imposed by the ECB on Greek banks[59], and the loss of national sovereignty.

The lack of liquidity has negative, especially, for Greece (where, it is used as a weapon of coercion and acceptance of the wrong policies imposed by the Troika), but rarely positive effects. One of the positive effects was that

56 See, Χαραλάμπου Ράπτη, <<Τελικός Γεωπολιτικός Στόχος τῆς Δύσεως: Ἐξαφανίσατε τοῦς Ὀρθοδόξους!>>, *Βοανεργές*, Ἀρ. Τεύχους 79, Μάϊος-Ἰούνιος 2015, 72-79.

57 EU through a system of subsidies destroyed the agriculture and livestock of Greece. Greece, a self-sufficient country in the past is importing, now, agricultural products and meet, milk and other products from the other EU member-nations. What a deceit is this union!

58 See, Bullard, Neely, and Wheelock (2009) call this risk as "systemic risk" (= the possibility that a triggering event, such as the failure of an individual firm, will seriously impair other firms or markets and harm the broader economy and the world economies). Also, Kallianiotis (2013b, 184-188).

59 See, http://www.nakedcapitalism.com/2015/07/the-coming-greek-bank-nationalization-bail-in-and-privatization.html.

speculators using borrowed money were being forced out of the market[60] or to use their own cash for their speculative games and not call money (borrowing). An increase oversight of the Treasuries and the central banks is needed, speculation must be curbed, and futures market has to be regulated because they affect the spot market with their outrageous scenarios and price manipulations. Employees in Brussels and CEO's salaries are provocative for our welfare and just societies; then, limits on officials and executive pay are necessary. Transparency and accountability for fraud or other greedy actions by politicians and executives is important for the public to start trusting the governments and the markets. Investment banks and exotic types of financial instruments must be regulated and the same must hold for all the other financial institutions. The government has to govern the country; otherwise, it will be beneficial for the country, the party in power to step down and allow another party to take over the administration of the nation.

Furthermore, these austerity measures, imposed by the Troika, have hit Greece particularly hard, considering that Greece had one of the most developed public sectors and the best welfare system among the European Union nations[61]. With the Greek government formerly being the largest employer in Greece, austerity actions (which include the privatization of large segments of the public portfolio, cuts to social services and "safety-net" benefits, and increases in taxes and tax collection) have left Greece with an unemployment rate of 27.3% (the highest in the EU)[62]. While the unemployment rate has improved slightly this year, researchers at the University of Portsmouth have found a correlation between the austerity measures and Greece's suicide rate, with 551 men killing themselves "solely because of fiscal austerity" between 2009 and 2010. The last two years, the suicide rate surged 35%. "That is almost one person per day. Given that in 2010 there were around two suicides in Greece per day, it appears 50% were due to austerity"[63]. Thus, the Troika's austerities are criminal policies against the citizens of Greece. Greek governments have also the responsibility for these crimes against their citizens and must give an account for all these events. Wolfgang Schäuble, the German Minister of Finance had the audacity

[60] *The Wall Street Journal*, September 17, 2008, pp. A1 and A16.

[61] This advanced social (pro humans) system was only in Greece, due to her value system and Hellenic-Orthodox tradition (equality among her citizens). There were no poor people in Greece before the current imposed debt crisis.

[62] In June 2015, it was 25.15%. See, http://www.tradingeconomics.com/greece/unemployment-rate.

[63] See, http://www.theguardian.com/world/2014/apr/21/austerity-greece-male-suicides-spending-cuts.

to say to the Greek Minister of Finance, Yanis Varoufakis that this program for Greece has been designed to fail[64].

HISTORY OF PRIVATIZATION IN EUROPE

The history of privatization dates from Ancient Greece, when governments contracted out many public services to the private sector (wealthy citizens, e.g., trierarchy)[65]. In the Roman Empire private individuals

[64] <<Είναι μια πρόσφατη στιχομυθία μεταξύ του κ. Βαρουφάκη και του "κυρίου" Σόιμπλε. "Το πρόγραμμα που συμφωνήθηκε για την Ελλάδα δεν μπορεί να εφαρμοστεί, θα αποτύχει" του επισημαίνει ο Βαρουφάκης. Και ο Σόιμπλε απαντάει: "Γι' αυτό σχεδιάστηκε, για να αποτύχει." Αυτή η απάντηση υποδηλώνει ότι υπάρχει ένας κρυφός σχεδιασμός, μια "κρυφή ατζέντα" εκ μέρους της Γερμανίας, την οποία η ηγετική ομάδα της κυβέρνησης όχι μόνον γνωρίζει, αλλά και την έχει αποδεχτεί. Όλη η τακτική που ακολουθεί καθιστά ολοφάνερο το γεγονός αυτό. Στις 13.7.2015, ο οιονεί πρωθυπουργός της Ελλάδος αποδέχτηκε και υπέγραψε ένα βαρύτατο πρόγραμμα δημοσιονομικής πειθαρχίας, το Τρίτο Μνημόνιο. Όλοι όσοι το συναποφάσισαν γνωρίζουν ότι το πρόγραμμα αυτό "δεν βγαίνει," δηλαδή δε θα μπορέσει να εφαρμοστεί. Τότε ποια η σκοπιμότητά του και ποιο το επόμενο βήμα-η κρυφή ατζέντα - που έχουν σχεδιάσει για μας, χωρίς εμάς.>>. See, Κατερίνα Αλεξανδράτου-Χατζηθεοδώρου, «ΝΙΚΗ ΤΗΣ ΔΗΜΟΚΡΑΤΙΑΣ ΚΑΙ ΝΕΟ ΣΥΝΤΑΓΜΑ», Εκδ. Γκοβόστη, 2014. Πηγή: http://www.logiosermis.net/.

[65] A Trierarchy (τριηραρχία) was a debt similar to a tax, and a duty similar to being conscripted, in the Navy of ancient Athens; this type of obligation was called a liturgy (λειτουργία). The person (or persons) up on whom the duty fell is called a Trierarch. The Trierarch was responsible for the outfitting, maintenance, operation and leadership of a warship known as a trireme (τριήρης, ancient Greek or Roman galley or warship having three tiers of oars on each side), the hull and mast of the ship are provided by the State. The responsibility could be that of one person or a combination of persons known as a syntrierarchy (συντριηραρχία). The cost of a whole Trierarchy was not less than forty minas (μνᾶ) nor more than a talent (τάλαντον) with the average being 50 mimas. The responsibility of the Trierarchy as a liturgy was so great that during some eras no other liturgy could be assessed in the same or the following year. The mina (also mna, μνᾶ) was an ancient Near Eastern unit of weight equivalent to 60 (50) shekels (the basic unit of money in Israel). The mina, like the shekel, was also a unit of currency. In ancient Greece originally had a weight of seventy (70) drachmae (δραχμαί), and later was increased to one hundred (100) drachmae. In the first century A.D., it amounted to about a fourth (1/4) of the wages earned annually by an agricultural worker (thus, they earned 400 Drs. per year). The Attic talent ('Αττικόν τάλαντον, a talent of the Attic standard), also known as the Athenian talent or Greek talent (τάλαντον, *talanton*), was an ancient unit of mass equal to 26 kg, as well as a unit of value equal to this amount of pure silver. A talent was originally intended to be the mass of water required to fill an amphora (39 liters, or approximately 39 kilograms of water). At the (12/22/2014) price of $15.46/oz, a silver talent is worth $14,178.72158. It was equivalent to 60 minae, 6,000 drachmae or 36,000 oboloi (ὀβολοί). The obol (ὀβολός *obolos*, literally "spit, iron rod" plural: ὀβολοί *oboloí*; hence also obolus, obolos) was an ancient silver coin. In Classical Athens, there were six obols to the drachma (literally "handful"); it could be exchanged for eight *chalkoi* (χαλκοί "copper pieces"). Two obols made a *diobol*, weighing around 1.41-1.43 grams of silver. *Triobols* were also in use. See, Kallianiotis (2015a).

and companies performed the majority of services including tax collection (tax farming)[66], army supplies (military contractors)[67], religious sacrifices, and construction. The same proceedings continued in the Byzantine (Hellenic Medieval) Empire. However, the Roman Empire had also created state-owned enterprises (SOEs), i.e., much of the grain was eventually produced on estates owned by the Emperor. Some scholars suggest that the cost of bureaucracy was one of the reasons for the fall of the Roman Empire[68]. In Britain, the privatization of common lands is referred to as enclosure (in Scotland as the Lowland Clearances and the Highland Clearances, in Greece as *perifraxis*, περίφραξις). Significant privatizations of this nature occurred from 1760 to 1820, coincident with the industrial revolution in that country.

Unfortunately, the last 30 years, privatization has become the only trend[69], even though that has been economically and politically disruptive. "More than 80 countries have launched ambitious efforts to privatize their state-owned enterprises. Since 1980, more than 2,000 state-owned enterprises (SOEs) have been privatized in developing countries, 6,800 worldwide"[70]. The total value of worldwide privatizations exceeded $185 billion by 1990 and the privatizations only in Europe and Central Asia between 1990 and 2006

---

[66] *Farming* is a technique of financial management, namely the process of commuting (changing), by its assignment by legal contract to a third party, a future uncertain revenue stream into fixed and certain periodic rents, in consideration for which commutation a discount in value received is suffered. It is most commonly used in the field of public finance, where the state wishes to gain some certainty about its future taxation revenue for the purposes of medium-term budgeting of expenditure. The tax collection process requires considerable expenditure on administration and the yield is uncertain both as to amount and timing, as taxpayers delay or default on their assessed obligations, often the result of unforeseen external forces such as bad weather affecting harvests. Governments (the lessors) have thus frequently over history resorted to the services of an entrepreneurial financier (the tenant) to whom they lease or assign the right to collect and retain the whole of the tax revenue due to the state in return for his payment into the Treasury of fixed sums (rent) in exchange.

[67] A *defense contractor* (or *private military contractor*) is a business organization or individual that provides products or services to a military department of a government. Products typically include military aircraft, ships, vehicles, weaponry, and electronic systems. Services can include logistics, technical support and training communications support, and in some cases team-based engineering in cooperation with the government. Military contractors do not generally provide direct support of military operations. Unfortunately, lately, we saw their corruption, the sales of needless and useless military equipment, and the bribery (commissions) that these military contractors offer to politicians. See, "How they Made Greece 'a Rubbish Dump of Armaments,' " *Dailynews24.gr*, September 4, 2012.

[68] But, this is not true; the Western Roman Empire fell because it was occupied by different barbaric Germanic tribes.

[69] See, http://data.worldbank.org/data-catalog/privatization-database.

[70] See, Kikeri, Nellis, and Shirley (1992).

exceeded $207 billion[71]. From 1988 to 1999, we had 8,342 privatizations and from 2000 to 2008 the number fell to 1,859 privatizations in developing countries, according to World Bank[72]. In 2008 privatizations in developing countries fell to $38 billion (down 70% from 2007). Privatization slowed because the global financial crisis took place, the stock markets reach a trough, and political difficulties continue even today (end of 2015). In 2009, privatization was increasing because the budget deficits were growing and new pressures for privatizations were imposed on these indebted countries. Ten countries accounted for nearly 90% of total value[73]. China, Russia, and Turkey together generated nearly 65% of total value in 2008. In Europe, there are privatizations in Serbia, Poland, Greece, and in other countries, too[74]. Europe and Central Asia raised $16.7 billion in 2008, down 60% from 2007; when, two Russian banking IPOs alone raised an equivalent amount. Serbia generated $1 billion and expanded its share from less than 0.5% in 2007 to 6%. Poland had 6% increase from IPO of ENEA, S.A. and Romania privatized Electrica Muntenia Sud.

Governments, especially those in Euro-zone that are in debt crises, want revenue and they are forced to sell any assets that the country had accumulated; but, there is another reason, in some cases, public workers acting unethically have reduced their productivity close to zero. This sell-off tension is a short-term objective of most privatization programs to generate some revenue collection for the current governments because private businesses do not pay taxes[75] and the pressure from the Troika (European Commission,

---

[71] See, Private Participation in Infrastructure Database, *The World Bank Group*.

[72] See, http://web.worldbank.org/WBSITE/EXTERNAL/TOPICS/EXTFINANCI ALSECTOR/0, content MDK:22936580~menuPK:7994350~pagePK:210058 ~piPK: 210062~ theSitePK: 282885,00.html.

[73] See, http://www.privatizationbarometer.net/.

[74] See, https://www.dbresearch.com/PROD/DBR_INTERNET_EN-PROD/PROD000000000 0318583/Privatisation+in+the+euro+area%3A++Differing+attitud.pdf.

[75] Actually, corporations and wealthy people are paying relatively less taxes compared to the middle class, which is unfair and unethical and their tax evasion, tax avoidance, and tax diversions are very high, too. This illegal capital fly is a large proportion of deposits in offshore centers and tax havens. Companies have become all too astute at paying for loopholes, which allow them to shift profits abroad or move their gains (on paper) to foreign low-tax/no-tax nations. There is no hope with these politicians, who care only for their politics and not for their citizens. The current "democratic" system does not work anymore! See, http://www.epi.org/publication/how-to-tax-multinational-corporations/. There is a need for major structural changes; otherwise, the future is invisible and aorist. Also, http://www.boston.com/business/globe/articles/2004/04/11/most_us_firms_paid_no_ income_taxes_in_90s/. And http://www.ritholtz.com/blog/2011/04/corporate-tax-rates-then-and-now/. Pfizer acquired Ireland's Allergan for $100 billion to lower US corporate tax liability. See, The Wall Street Journal, October 30, 2015, pp. A1 and A2.

ECB, and IMF) to reduce budget deficits and national debts is unbearable. Also, the liberalization policies, the deregulation, and the globalization of the financial system, lately, try to increase supply and demand of securities in the domestic capital markets and integrate them with the EU and the international one; therefore, privatization is the main contributor of financial assets[76]. The Nordic countries and Greece lagged a little behind compared to the rest of Europe, but the last 30 years the socialists (PASOK) and the "centrists" (N.D.) and recently the followers of the memoranda (μνημονιακοί) in Greece are selling almost everything[77]. In terms of industries, the most intense activity was in the telecommunications, financial services, transport, and public utilities sectors. The Maastricht treaty provides (imposes) a unique "motivation" for privatization in the entire EU[78]. But, privatizations in Europe have caused many serious problems to Europeans[79].

Indisputably, certain public goods and services should remain primarily in the hands of governments in order to ensure that everyone in the society has access to them (such as law enforcement, the security of the nation, basic health care, the investment in human capital, the basic education, the water[80], and many others). Likewise, private goods and services should remain in the hands of the private sector, controlled by the government through regulations and a fair tax system. There is a positive externality, when the government provides public goods and services to society at large, such as defense and disease control. The government has to run these SOEs as efficient as the private sector. As for natural monopolies, many claim that they are subject to

---

[76] See, http://www.theglobalist.com/why-europe-needs-to-put-privatization-back-on-the-agenda/.

[77] Demonstrations were much more often lately, due to the austerity measures, privatizations, and loss of jobs. The goal of the Troika is a huge reduction of the public sector and its employees. The party in power in Greece was the socialist, which became more liberal than the traditional centrist (N.D.) one (TV News, 2010 and 2011). Then, a coalition government followed the same orders, too. And lately, a leftish party (SYRIZA) was forced to sign the third memorandum of austerity, to sell-off of public wealth, and to contribute to the social misery. The Troika subdued even the leftish parties; what has been left uninfluenced, at the moment, in Europe are the nationalist parties (πατριωτικά κόμματα).

[78] See, Privatizations in Europe by country. https://en.wikipedia.org/wiki/List_of_privatizations These Greek leaders have to say sometimes "NO" because Greece has lost its public wealth, its sovereignty and it is losing her own identity, too. There is no need for Greece to be a member of a union with culture and value system inferior of her own. This is the biggest historical mistake of Hellenism and responsible are her leaders, who act against Greece's interest. Of course, if the Bank of Greece was a public bank (SOE) and drachma the currency of the country, the current crisis would have been shallow.

[79] See, http://www.redpepper.org.uk/Privatisation-in-Europe/.

[80] See, http://www.dw.com/en/privatization-of-water-in-europe-controversial/a-16605658. See also, http://www.mintpressnews.com/eu-commissions-insistence-on-privatization-of-water-services-reveals-double-standards/39321/.

unfair competition, and they can be better administrated by the state. Citizens of the European nations are responsible to elect an effective and uncorrupted government.

History of Privatization in Greece

The purpose, in this section, is to examine this vague "intellectual" debate, which is very common in EU and especially in Greece, about her forced privatizations and their effects on her debt, on financial markets, and about the kinds of activities that belong in the public sector and the private one. But, no one can trust the controlled EU anymore; even, the Czech President Klaus assailed the EU as undemocratic and said it should halt further centralization of powers[81]. Troika is forcing Greece to sell public enterprises and derive €50 billion from these sales[82]; otherwise, there would be restrictions on the future installments of the bailout loans that had been approved in 2010[83] of €110 billion, a second one of €173 billion in March 2012, and a third one of €86 billion with the new third memorandum in August 2015[84]. Thus, currently, with the pressure from Troika, Greece has to privatize SOEs to collect these €50 billion, but the market is at a very bad financial distress (undervalued). Then, the Greek SOEs will be sold at a very low price (fire sales), which means negligible revenue for the government. Now, the Greek government and the Quartet (European Parliament, European Commission, ECB, and IMF)[85] of the country's creditors on Friday, August 7, 2015, agreed on the terms of setting up a new privatization fund, which will replace the existing Hellenic Republic Asset Development Fund (HRADF), thus concluding a part

[81] See, *The Wall Street Journal*, February 20, 2009, pp. A1 and A11.

[82] See, http://www.huffingtonpost.com/yanis-varoufakis/privatization-plan-greece-europe_b_7836684.html Also, http://www.project-syndicate.org/commentary/greece-privatization-plan-public-assets-by-yanis-varoufakis-2015-07.

[83] See, Kallianiotis (2011a).

[84] See, https://en.wikipedia.org/wiki/Greek_government-debt_crisis. Also, http://yanisvaroufakis.eu/2015/08/17/greeces-third-mou-memorandum-of-understading-annotated-by-yanis-varoufakis/.

[85] On August 19, 2015, Greek Prime Minister Alexis Tsipras called for the European Parliament to join the so-called *quartet of creditor institutions* overseeing the country's €86 billion EU/IMF bailout program. "I deem it politically imperative that the sole European institution with direct popular mandate acts as the ultimate guarantor of democratic accountability and compatibility of economic policy in Europe," Tsipras wrote in a letter to European Parliament President Martin Schulz. See, http://www.theguardian.com/business/blog/live/2015/jul/31/troika-talks-in-greece-overshadowed-by-imf-bombshell-business-live#block-55bb78f0e4b0b88df60f9b8c.

of the negotiating agenda. Finance ministry officials told ANA-MPA that the agreement envisages the set-up of a fund, which will create a reserve of assets worth €50 billion in the next 30 years. This is a true expropriation of the national wealth[86].

Between 1991 and 2006, Greece had implemented 61 transactions worth over $20 billion of privatization revenues. Privatization in Greece began in the early 1990s after the first election of the New Democracy Party. The government considered privatization as the main policy objcctive, and issued a list of firms to be privatized. The initial stage of the Greek privatization program mainly involved the enterprises belonging to the IRO. The first transactions date back to 1991 and 1992 with the full sales of the Olympic Marine shipping company, the Bank of Chios, and of Elvim (Heracles Gen Cement). However, the implementation of this first wave of privatizations was blocked by strong political and labor union opposition. The context changed after 1995, when Greece was admitted to candidacy in the European Economic and Monetary Union (EMU). This was an exerted pressure on the governments to implement structural reforms in order to foster policy credibility. Indeed, after a break lasting three years, the divestment process resumed in 1996 and gathered momentum through the second half of the 1990s onwards. During this second stage, which continues to the present, privatizations mainly involved the public utilities, services, and telecommunications. After 2011, everything is for sale in Greece with the European pressure from the three inhumane memoranda[87].

In March 1996, telecommunications started being privatized with the initial public offer of Hellenic Telecommunications Organization (OTE), with an offer of 7.6% of its shares. Subsequent sales of the telecommunication group occurred in 1997 (12.4% of capital sold), in 1998 through 2005 two tranches of 3.5% and 15% of capital, respectively, were sold. In 2007, the Greek State sold 10.7% of OTE share capital to institutional investors. Deutsche Telekom signs a shareholder agreement with the Greek government, via which, as of November 5, 2008, each has a 25% stake plus one share in OTE share capital. In 2009, an additional 5% of Greek State shares, including voting rights, are sold, bringing Deutsche Telekom's stake to 30%. To date 70.6% of its capital has been sold, raising over $5.6 billion. The Greek State's participation is not at 20%. In March 2009, OTE sold its mobile phone unit

[86] See, Cobus de Swardt, "Money will End up to the Pockets of the Few…," *Dailynews24.gr*, September 20, 2012. Also, http://greece.greekreporter.com/2015/08/08/greece-creditors-agree-on-creation-of-new-privatization-fund/.

[87] See, http://greece.greekreporter.com/?s=privatization.

Cosmofon for €190 million to Slovenia's Telekom. The deal also included Cosmofon's main distribution network "Germanos Telekom Skopje" with its 66 stores. In 2011 OTE signed agreement with Telekom Srbija to sell its 20% stake in the company for €380 million. Also it Launches satellite Pay TV services under the brand name OTE TV. Deutsche Telekom acquired extra 10% of OTE share capital raising its stake to 40%. In 2013, OTE announced the signing of an agreement to sell its 100% stake in Cosmo Bulgaria Mobile EAD (Globul) and Germanos Telecom Bulgaria (Germanos) to Telenor, the Norwegian telecom operator. The agreement consideration reached €717 million (enterprise value). Also, in the same year, it announced the signing of an agreement to sell its 99.05% stake in Hellas Sat, to Arabsat, for €208 million, plus 7 million in dividends.

Other transactions included the sale of 16% of the National Bank of Greece, which happened between 1998 and 1999. Then, the three subsequent issues of the state power producer, Public Power Corporation (PPC, ΔΕΗ), took place, respectively in 2001, 2003[88], and 2005 and worth overall about $1.4 billion. In addition, the four tranches of the Greek Organization of Football Prognostics (OPAP) in 2001, 2002, 2003 and 2005, worth in total $2.75 billion. The most proceeds were raised from the privatization of telecommunications (41% of total revenues) and of public utilities (21% of total revenues), such as water supply (i.e., the privatization of the Water Supply & Sewerage System in 1999), electric, gas, and water distribution (i.e., the sale of the Gas supply company of Thessaloniki EPA in 2000), and the already mentioned electricity sector [i.e., Public Power Corporation, PPC (ΔΕΗ)].

Also, the financial sector has raised 16% of total revenues. Among the commercial banks, investment banks, and holding companies, privatized are: the Bank of Chios in 1991, the Bank of Athens in 1993, the Athens Bourse in 1997, the General Hellenic Bank in 1998 and 2004, the National Bank of Greece in 1998, 1999, 2003 and 2004, the Hellenic Industrial Development Bank in 1999, the Greek Stock Exchange Holdings in 2000, and finally, the

[88] This was the period of Costas Semites, as Prime Minister, who put Greece to Euro-zone and this anti-Greek choice will make Greece to pay an enormous social cost for generations to come. Germany is controlling Greece since 1832, when Otto, also spelled Otho (Ὄθων, Βασιλεὺς τῆς Ἑλλάδος) a Bavarian prince, became the first modern King of Greece under the Convention of London and he started the destruction of the Hellenic-Orthodox civilization that it is continued today with the EU (modern Germany). See, Kallianiotis (2015c).

Agricultural Bank of Greece[89] in 2000. In addition, privatization of the state-owned enterprises (SOEs) was one of the goals of the Kostas Karamanlis' Government. In his Platform Speech (March 2004), he said that "Government will reduce its business activities, give up its role as a contractor and enhance its regulatory powers. At all events, it will maintain control on the natural monopolies of transport networks." The first move was the sell-off in 2004 of an 8.2% stake in Hellenic Petroleum for around $240 million. Then, DEKA, the Greek state portfolio management agency, sold its stake to a unit of the Latsis Group. In November 2004, a 7.46% stake in National Bank of Greece was placed with foreign and Greek institutional investors via an accelerated book-building process. Revenues were worth the insignificant amount around $725 million. All these SOEs had enormous assets, but the buyers were paying only a very low price, due to their depressed market value per share. Those irresponsible politicians have to give an account to the Greek citizens for their endless mistakes. Al least, now, these parties are out of the government, but they are in Parliament as opposition parties (N.D. and PASOK). The bad thing for Greece is that EU put SYRIZA inside the same trap, which was a big surprise for everyone and the biggest mistake for the party.

Furthermore, the goal of reducing budget deficit led the Government to plan an ambitious privatization program for 2005; it aimed to raise more than $2 billion in the year. In this context, in July 2005, a 16.4% of the gambling company OPAP was sold via a retail and institutional public offer, raising more than $1.5 billion. OPAP's (Lottery and Betting Monopoly) privatization completed in 2008, when the last remaining government-owned stock was sold. In September 2005, a 10% stake of the telecommunications company OTE was sold, via a public offer, generating revenues worth over $1 billion. The privatization process continued in 2006 with the IPO of Postal Savings Bank, whose 35% was sold on the Athens Stock Exchange for barely $800 million. The largest privatization, ever occurred in Greece, took place in the second half of 2006, with the complete sell off of Emporiki Bank. The government sold to Crédit Agricole its 35.56% stake, raising around $2.2 billion. Another "important" operation was the public offer of Hellenic Telecommunication Organization (OTE). In June 2007, the government, finally, sold a 10.07% stake for almost $1.5 billion, as part of its ambitious privatization program for the year, aimed at repaying the country's public debt. After a few days, in July 2007, the Greek government had completed

[89] The Agricultural Bank of Greece should have remained public to finance and support the farmers of the country. The primary sector of the country is necessary for the country side and the villages that prevent the loss of tradition of the nation.

another long-awaited operation: the sale of a 20% stake in Greek Postal Savings Bank for more than €500 million. With this operation, the Greek government once again, after the gratifying result of 2006, had reached its privatization revenues target, €1.7 billion, well in advance than year-end[90].

After these excessive privatizations, Deutsche Telekom AG gained control of Greece's phone company (Hellenic Telecommunications Organization, OTE), which created a goliath in the Balkans[91]. The German telecommunications company paid about €2.9 billion ($4.6 billion) for 25% of the shares of OTE and in 2011 it took the majority control of the company[92]. At the same time, OTE and Cosmote brought Deutsche Telekom access to Greece, Albania, Skopje, Serbia, Romania, and Bulgaria. Ten years earlier, in 2000, Deutsche Telekom had acquired a majority stake in Hungary's Magyar Telekom Telecommunications that gave it indirect control of telecom companies in Skopje and Montenegro. In 2001, Deutsche Telekom acquired a direct majority state in Croatia's Hrvatski Telekom. They have created a private monopolist in Balkans and the workers and customers in these countries have been negatively affected. This is also a very serious problem for the security of Greece, which is surrounded by so many enemies[93]. These are some of the negative effects of any irrationally enforced privatization.

---

[90] See, *Privatization Barometer*, http://www.privatizationbarometer.net/atlas.php?id=13&mn=PM&print=1.

[91] The government of PASOK had sold 66% of OTE and the government of N.D. sold the other 29%. Finally, only 5% of its shares stay with the Greek government. The conflicts in the Parliament were continuing for this issue and the demonstrations were going on for a long time (TV News *ALTER*, May 9, 2008). Polls revealed that 71.7% of Greeks were against OTE's privatization (*e-grammes.gr*, 11/14/2008). But, no one cares for the powerless citizens' opinion anymore. Globalization is terrorizing and crushing everything in its way to global control. The worse phenomenon is that it started the implementation of its program from the "powerful" US and continues with the "lost" EU. The other continents are not going to provide any resistance. The bad is that it started at the first day of the eighth millennium (ὀγδοῖται).

[92] See, Kallianiotis (2009). The Greek government was hoping to sell off up to all of its remaining 16% stake in OTE in June 2011, but did not make clear how much would be offered to Deutsche Telekom, which currently holds a 30% stake in the company. OTE shares closed up 4.8% on the Athens Stock Market, on May 26, 2011. See, http://www.msnbc.msn.com/id/43181917/ns/business-stocks_and_economy/t/greece-seeks-rapid-sale-ote-stake/#.

[93] The German magazine *Spiegel* published that Deutsche Telekom was accused for tapping phones (bugging telephones of Greek officials) during the agreement process with OTE. This was a criminal act and in the future the security of Greece will be in danger. In 2007, Vodafone was tapping telephones of many Greek leaders, from the Prime Minister, to the Chief of Staff of the Arm Forces, and many other members of the government, etc.; but unfortunately, the company was not expelled from the country. Politicians have zero power in our days!.. (TV News *ALTER*, May 26, 2008).

In March 2009, the Greek government "succeeded" to privatize the Greek airline carrier Olympic Airways[94] by selling it to Marfin Egnatia (MIG)[95] for €177.2 million. In a few days European Commission (EU) gave the approval of this privatization and the ratification took place from the Privatization Committee of the Greek government. The new owner, Andreas Vgenopoulos, said that he would spend €100 million to buy new airplanes and he was thinking to collaborate with Iberia; he kept the existing personnel of the carrier and he started accepting applications for new hiring of employees[96]; but then came the catastrophic debt crisis, the recession, and the imposed austerities from the Troika and all plans were changed[97].

---

[94] Greek airline, formerly known as Olympic Airways, founded on April 6, 1957, by the Greek ship-owner Aristotle Onassis (1906–1975); but, from 1975, wholly owned by the Greek government. Services from Greece into Western Europe began in 1957, and by 1980 services extended throughout Greece and internationally from Athens to many of the major cities of Europe and the Middle East, as well as to North America, Africa, Southeast Asia, and Australia. Since its privatization, the airline has disappeared from all its international routes and today, it is at its death door. What a pity for all this history!..

[95] There were three prospective bids (Aegean Airlines, Chrysler Aviation, and MIG); the government and the employees of Olympic Airways preferred MIG (Andreas Vgenopoulos) to buy the company and the deal was successful (TV News *ALTER*, March 4, 2009).

[96] In a press conference Vgenopoulos said that his objective was to keep this historic Greek airline in Greek heads for patriotic reasons. (TV News *ALTER*, March 10, 2009). On October 22, 2012, the Aegean announced a merger with Olympic, which was subject to EU competition clearance. See, http://www.ryanair.com/en/news/ryanair-welcomes-aegean-olympic-merger. The controlled EU is in "control" of everything in these poor member-nations.

[97] On March 6, 2009, Development Minister Kostis Hatzidakis announced the sale of the flight operations and the technical base companies to MIG. As a result, after 35 years of state control and ten years of failed sales attempts, it was hoped that Olympic will once again become a private corporation. The new owners promised to secure approximately 5000 of the 8500 jobs of the Group. But, on September 28, 2009, Olympic Airlines ceased to fly to most of their 69 destinations, maintaining flights to Tel Aviv, Beirut, Cairo and all public service obligation routes within Greece, until the Ministry for Transport and Communications redistributed the routes in late November, when Olympic Airlines entered liquidation. Existing passengers were accommodated on other airlines. Employees of the old company that were in destinations no longer served had been affected. The last Olympic Airlines flight was flight 424 from Toronto via Montreal, landing at 11:10 on September 29, 2009 at the Athens International Airport. Olympic Air took over the rest of the operations on September 29, 2009 and their first flight was on October 1, 2009 at 06:20 leaving the Athens International Airport and heading to Thessaloniki Makedonia Airport. On February 22, 2010, Olympic Air and its main competitor Aegean Airlines announced they had reached an agreement to merge their operations, phasing out the Aegean brand. After an inquiry by the European competitions commission, it was announced on January 26, 2011 that the merger was blocked citing anti-competitive concerns (*sic*). However, the sale to Aegean Airlines was eventually approved by the EU Competition Commission on October 10, 2013, and the airline is now a subsidiary of Aegean Airlines. It currently operates 14 *Bombardier Dash 8* aircrafts, its former fleet of *Airbus A320* and A319 aircraft having been

Later, this pressure from the Troika (which its intensions are suspicious) was forcing the previous Greek coalition governments (N.D. and PASOK) to sell every public asset (from seaports to airports to roads to islands and to all the national wealth) and to make up the requested by the Troika amount of €50 billion. The Fund of Utilization of the Private Property of the Public Sector (ΤΑΙΠΕΔ) had focused forty (40) uninhabited islands and plans to lease them, mostly, to foreign investors for 50 years that they can exploit them by creating tourist facilities. This office (ΤΑΙΠΕΔ) was examining 562 from the 6,000 islands that are under Greek possession to exploit them[98]. But, this pro-memorandum coalition government lost the elections in January 25, 2015 and some public wealth might be saved to be bequeath to the future generations, where it belongs.

Some other obnoxious sales are the followings. The Turkish businessman Mehmet Karadinch opened a Turkish bath on the island of Kos (Dodecanese) and young Greek workers found employment, there (sic). Also, other Turkish businessmen are planning to build a casino on the island of Chios. This will be the second destruction of the island by the same people[99]. Another incredible sell off was the sale of a Greek island to Israel to use it for exercises and training of its military navy; but, thank God, the agreement did not go through. At the end, the Ministry of Defense of Israel rejected this idea as economically unfavorable[100]. This is occupation of the country and these ignorant Greek officials, who take these decisions, are very dangerous for the security of the country and must be expel not only from their post, but from the country, too. A new austerity bill ("multi-law"), which included the latest cuts on wages, salaries, and pensions received 153 votes from the Greek Parliament at the early morning on November 8, 2012[101].

The new third memorandum (August 2015) requires many more privatizations[102]. From these SOEs that are the target of the Quartet, 14

sold during the various processes covered above. What an inglorious termination of these suspicious privatizations!

[98] See, "For sale off the first forty islands," *Dailynews24.gr*, September 12, 2012.

[99] The first one was in 1822, the devastation and massacre of Chios by the forefathers of today investors. The casino will destroy the island financially, morally, and ethically, too. See, *Dailynews24.gr*, September 13, 2012.

[100] See, "Defense Officials: Barak mulled buying Greek isle for Israeli navy training," *Dailynews24.gr*, September 12, 2012.

[101] See, "153 'Yes' and 7 cross-outs from PASOK and ND," *Dailynews24.rg*, November 8, 2012.

[102] See, http://unionsforenergydemocracy.org/third-memorandum-or-grexit-what-are-the-implications-for-the-future-of-greeces-energy-system/.

peripheral airports[103] are at the aim of Germany to buy them (a German public firm, *Fraport AG*); then, this is not even privatization, it is expropriation of the Greek public wealth by the German public sector. This new memorandum is particularly concerned about restructuring Greece's energy sector through further privatizations. There have been a number of EU directives in the past 10-15 years that were designed to make electricity markets "competitive" by breaking up ("unbundling") what were once fully public natural monopolies. This process was set in motion by the EU's directive on the Internal Energy Market for Electricity and Gas passed down to member states in 1996. Therefore one of the main targets for privatization is the Public Power Corporation (PPC, ΔΕΗ). So far 49% of the PPC has already been privatized as a result of the EU directives, but the Greek nation is still in control of 51% of the PPC, which is Greece's largest company. It owns almost all of the country's installed power capacity (generated by lignite, oil, hydroelectric and natural gas power plants). The PPC is a big target for the privatizers (MNCs). Under the previous government (N.D.), privatization of the electricity system was being fast-tracked in accordance with the conditions laid down by the Troika's previous memorandum. However, the day after the election of SYRIZA on January 25, 2015, the privatization of the PPC was halted[104]; but, we do not know for how long.

Now, the Third Memorandum has put the PPC's privatization firmly back on the agenda, and Hellenic Petroleum and offshore oil or natural gas drilling parcels are also likely targets for a sell-off. The Memorandum also specifically demands "the privatization of the electricity transmission network operator (ADMIE)." Aside from leading to the sell-off of state assets (public wealth) to repay a (small) portion of the debt (€10-€12 billion), the Memorandum will perpetuate Greece's dependency on imported fossil fuels, and any offshore drilling for oil and gas will be performed by multinationals largely for the benefit of multinationals, as has been the case with the UK[105]. N.D.

---

[103] See, http://www.dailymail.co.uk/news/article-3202393/Greek-Prime-Minister-reneges-pre-election-promise-not-privatise-indebted-country-s-infrastructure-selling-14-airports-German-company.html. Unfortunately, on December 14, 2015, Germany bought these 14 airports. (TV News *ALPHA*, 12/14/2015).

[104] The SYRIZA-led government was against an Energy Union that undermines Greece's national interests, including in its relations with Russia, said Greek energy minister Panagiotis Lafazanis, who also ruled out any privatization schemes for the country's energy sector. See, http://www.euractiv.com/sections/energy/athens-opposes-eu-energy-strategy-blocks-privatizations-313102. But, the anti-democratic EU forced him out of the SYRIZA party and out of the government.

[105] In the UK, six private corporations (just only one of them British) dominate the power generation sector and 57% of fuel used to generate electricity is imported.

government and the multinationals were developing plans for more fossil fuel exploitation in the eastern Mediterranean, south of Crete and in the Ionian Sea. In Aegean Sea, Greece has the "visitors of history," the Turks that cause serious problems with oil exploitations. In terms of energy, the "invisible zones" seem particularly illusive because of the nature of a present system characterized by import dependency and the presently large role of the PPC, which has been targeted for privatization under the Memorandum. In other sectors, such as farming[106] and food distribution, provision of health services, the utilization of unused skills, etc., actions in these zones could begin to make "important changes and improvements" (which will bankrupt small businesses and cause higher unemployment in the country).

Further, Yanis Varoufakis (the former Finance Minister of Greece) said that on July 12, 2015, the Summit of Euro-zone leaders dictated its terms of surrender the Greek Prime Minister Alexis Tsipras. One of these terms concerned the disposition of Greece's remaining public assets[107]. EU (actually, Germany) forces the Greek government to privatize much of the country's state-owned facilities, including rail and road transportation systems, air and seaports, utilities and publicly-owned real estate holdings. Under the proposed privatization plan in 2014, the Greek government would sell 49% of the stakes in state railway operator OSE (ΟΣΕ); sell off all state-run casinos; sell off minority stakes in the Hellenic Post (Ἑλληνικόν Ταχυδρομεῖον), Thessaloniki water utility EYATH, and Athens water and sewage utility EYDAP (ΕΥΔΑΠ)[108]; create new private-public partnerships for infrastructure projects, such as the construction and operation of new highways; and issue new gaming licenses toward developing the "gaming and Internet betting industry." Now, the Troika is insisting on these privatization schemes and many new ones, as a condition for much-needed loans to bail out the Greek government; but only if the country could demonstrate that it could potentially stabilize its economy and repay the loans. EU is mocking Greece and her politicians are submitted without any conditions.

---

[106] Farmers announced that they will start very soon a series of mobilizations, with closing the highways and demonstrations against the measures that the government is planning to take for them (TV News *MEGA*, October 11, 2015).

[107] See, http://www.project-syndicate.org/commentary/greece-privatization-plan-public-assets-by-yanis-varoufakis-2015-07.

[108] See, http://multinationales.org/Forced-Privatizations-in-Greece. Also, https://www.theparliamentmagazine.eu/articles/opinion/eu-commission-failed-properly-address-citizens-water-privatisation-fears. And, http://www.truth-out.org/news/item/32499-leaked-eu-memorandum-reveals-renewed-attempt-at-imposing-water-privatization-on-greece.

Polychroniou (2014)[109] pointed out that the Greek privatization plan's administrator, the Hellenic Republic Asset Development Fund (TAIPED), resembles Germany's Treuhandanstalt, the agency charged with the privatization of East Germany's state-owned enterprises following unification. Treuhandanstalt was accused of turning over to West German big business hundreds of billions Deutsche Marks in national property for little or nothing. This created a deficit of DM300 billion (equal to over $206 billion, today) that dragged East Germany's 1992 industrial production down to a third of 1989's figure. Meanwhile, one in every two industrial jobs was lost, female unemployment hit 65%, the crime rate spiked by 300% spike, and the national birth and marriage rates dropped to 55% and 50%, respectively. A number of Treuhandanstalt managers were ultimately indicted for corruption and embezzlement. Also, with TAIPED being an extra-legal organization imposed upon the Greek government by the international community, its authority is not based on Greek law, but on international treaty. And as TAIPED's board of directors also has close links with the financial sectors, the possibility of gross economic misconduct, cronyism, and illegal transactions are higher than they were in East Germany under Treuhandanstalt. Then, the country is entering in new misadventures[110].

Also, "Prior to 2010, the value of Greek state-owned assets was estimated to be worth €280 billion. The first bailout plan estimated the value of Greek state-owned assets to be worth €50 billion. Three years later, the Greek government seems to have found the Troika's estimates extremely high and expects that the revenues generated through the privatization efforts of TAIPED will reach about €20 billion by 2020"[111]. This is a big fraud against Greeks and their public wealth by the corrupted partners in Europe. With plans to privatize much of Greece's public wealth continuously being developed and debated, such as a bill submitted in May 2015 that would convert much of Greece's protected coastal areas into "composite tourist villages"; questions concerning the side effects of austerity are being ignored. These "dangers" theoretically would include tax frauds and other perceived "threats" to Greece's economic recovery. Greeks are increasingly asking who, exactly, is benefiting from Greece's newfound "stability" (write complete instability and

---

109 See, http://www.truth-out.org/news/item/25244-greece-a-nation-for-sale-and-the-death-of-democracy. How is it possible assets with value of €280 billion to be sold for €20 billion?

110 West Germans took advantage of the German reunification and exploited their own race, the East Germans. Then, why are we surprised of what they are doing to Greece and the rest of Europe?

111 See also, http://www.truth-out.org/news/item/25244-greece-a-nation-for-sale-and-the-death-of-democracy.

chaos). The new privatization fund will replace the existing Hellenic Republic Asset Development Fund (HRADF) and the new agreement envisages the set-up of a Fund, which creates a reserve of assets of €50 billion in the next 30 years. The Fund will include state assets, state enterprises' shares, infrastructure, and real estate assets, with the option of including future revenues from the utilization of natural resources (i.e., hydrocarbon). Out of €50 billion of assets in the Fund, 50% will be used as bank collateral (€25 billion will be needed depending on banks' recapitalization needs), while the remaining 50% will be distributed to growth (25%) and debt servicing (25%). The new Fund will be based in Athens, it will be controlled by the Greek government, while the European Commission will have a supervisory role[112]. Thus, unregulated banks are the biggest problem in our corrupted financial system.

In Greece, four years ago, a voted Law 3986/2011 entitled "Urgent Measures for the Application of the Midterm Framework for the Fiscal and Financial Strategy 2012-2015" was another and most resounding effort of the Greek government to persuade its creditors (the Troika) that it was determined to tackle its public debt crisis; but creditors continued to mistrust the Greek government. Its most significant innovation was the establishment of a Fund for the selling-off of assets belonging to the Greek nation (public wealth). In particular, the portfolio of the Greek State comprises four different categories of assets: (a) public enterprises, (b) infrastructures, (c) state monopoly rights, and (d) real property. Such assets were to be "exploited" pursuant to the (so defined in the Law) Operational Strategy for the exploitation of the assets of the Fund; a program to be elaborated in accordance with the provisions of the Midterm Framework for the fiscal and financial Strategy 2012-2015, divided into indicative quarterly goals.

This Midterm Framework predicted the same aggregate income of €50 billion for Greece faster than the latest one within a period of five years (2011-2015) through a series of privatizations. The goal was to sell off these assets openly and transparently, in a fair market price; and the hope behind this effort, to decrease public debt by 20% of the GDP. Starting from the second quarter of 2011, the privatizations program included a vast number of state activities; some of them reserved until that time for the Greek nation solely: (1) transport and infrastructures, (2) ports[113], (3) water supply and sewerage

[112] See, *ana-mpa*. http://greece.greekreporter.com/2015/08/08/greece-creditors-agree-on-creation-of-new-privatization-fund/.

[113] See, http://www.keeptalkinggreece.com/2013/10/10/troika-wants-to-close-down-22-greek-airports-after-lufthansas-recommendation/.

services, (4) betting and gaming, (5) the energy sector, (6) telecommunications and postal services, (7) defense industry, (8) banking industry, (9) mining enterprises and mines, and (10) real property[114]. Greece is in serious financial, social, and political distress, with her mistakes to join EMU, the enormous debts and deficits, the tax avoidance, evasion, and diversion, the corruption, the embezzlement, the socialists in power since 1980 and the "pseudo-conservatives" for some years, and now (after the elections of September 20, 2015) the disappointing SYRIZA and ANEL in government, also with three memoranda that have increased the pressure from Troika to sell off its public wealth, which will affect negatively the social welfare of the nation. The country, the government, and the poor citizens are in big trouble, except if they will leave the oppressive Euro-zone.

Many people (economists from all over the world and simple Greek citizens) also were warning against the privatization (confiscation of the national wealth) practices, due to the inherent tendency toward corruption, deceptions, embezzlements, and undervaluation of the assets, especially after 1974. In many areas, in which the government could provide services are essentially profitless; the only way private companies could, to any degree, operate them would be through contracts or block payments. In these cases, the private firm's performance in a particular project would be removed from their performance, and embezzlement and dangerous cost-cutting measures might be taken to maximize profits. The corruption in Greece became scientific after the takeover of the country by the PASOK party (not even a party, but a "movement" as they call themselves) in 1980. Kostas Mitsotakis in a speech, in the Greek parliament in 1994, had predicted the forthcoming crisis that the PASOK party was bringing to the country[115]. Then, Costas Semites came (was brought by the dark powers) in power and continued with the demolition of what Andreas Papandreou had forgotten to destroy. Greece, today, does not remind anything of what this great traditional value-oriented nation was before 1974 because N.D. contributed to the destruction of the country, too.

In addition, as Stiglitz (2002, 54-58) has stressed, from his work experience in government and international organizations, that the IMF and the World Bank [even the EU] have approached the privatization issue from a narrow ideological perspective (privatization was to be pursued rapidly). Also, scorecards were kept for the countries making the transition from public to

[114] See, http://skift.com/2013/05/28/greeces-ports-trains-and-airports-are-up-for-grabs/.

[115] See, *Dailynews24.gr*, 24/1/2012, video with Mitsotakis' speech.

private ownership (from communism to the market economy, actually, to the repulsive globalization)[116]. Those who privatized faster were given the high marks. Through these pressures, privatization often did not bring the benefits that were promised. "The problems that arose from these failures have created antipathy to the very idea of privatization"[117]. The IMF, EU, and other international institutions assume that markets arise quickly to meet every need, but in fact, only government activities arise; free markets have failed to provide essential services because they act pro-cyclically[118] and against the real sector of the economy. This is obvious everywhere outside the United States. Economists and political advisors, who have studied in US universities, try to impose the same theories and policies on their countries[119], but, these do not work because the structure of the economies, the culture, and the needs of the citizens are different, there.

Further, the private financial markets are also very risky and they have a negative effect on individuals' lives; for this reason a healthy public system must exist (like, the Social Security, IKA, the Unemployment Insurance, Public Education, Public Health care). Eliminating the government enterprises may cause security problems (i.e., utilities, telephone, education, peripheral airports on borderlands, etc.), unemployment, and other types of suffering to the citizens, especially with the creation of private monopolies. Drogalis (2008) criticizes the American social welfare system comparing it with the supreme Aristotle's social welfare one. The same can be said for the European Union and Greece, which follow the US (a general servile imperialism). Aristotle recommended that the state must gather together all "excess revenue"

[116] "From the skylla (ruthless bitch) to charybdis (predatory monster)." Many members of the EU from the previous Soviet Republics contemplate communism instead of the current global financial crisis of capitalism, as we see often in the News.

[117] See, Stiglitz (2002, 54).

[118] IMF continues even today, with the global financial crisis, the Euro-zone debt crises, and the severe recessions, to insist on the same wrong philosophy: High taxes, lower wages and salaries, privatizations, and tough austerity measures to reduce the deficits and debts ("internal devaluation"). But, the ultimate economic objective is the social welfare of the citizens and not the welfare of the government Treasury or of the lenders or of the speculators. See, Kallianiotis (2013a, 44-45) for IMF's criticisms.

[119] An example of this problem is the following. The governors in many central banks around the world were coming from MIT and were students of Stanley Fischer. (1) Stanley Fischer (ex-governor Bank of Israel and now, vice-chairman of the US Fed), (2) Ben S. Bernanke (ex-governor US Fed), (3) Mario Draghi (governor ECB), (4) Mervyn King (governor Bank of England), (5) Lucas Papademos (ex-governor of Bank of Greece, ex-ECB vice president, and ex-prime minister of Greece), (6) Athanassios Orphanides (ex-governor Bank of Cyprus), (7) Duwuri Subbarao (governor Reserve Bank of India), (8) Jose De Gregorio (Central Bank of Chile), (9) Charles Bean (King's deputy in Bank of England), and (10) Oliver Blanchard (IMF). The club of central bankers (sic).

into a fund and distribute this wealth through block grants "sufficient for the purchase of a plot of land" or "enough to start men in commerce or agriculture" (1320a 39-46). Today, the Greek government acts against its own ancestors and its civilization by taking away (expropriate) all the wealth from the state (from the tax payers-citizens) with privatizations. Thus, if the current Greek government (SYRIZA-ANEL) will follow the same steps, as its predecessors, it will destroy (sell off to foreigners) the public wealth of the future generations, which is completely unethical and illegal and they will never win any elections in the future.

Unfortunately, the previous Greek authorities believed (had been persuaded by some special-interest groups or forced by the EU and the IMF) that it was important to privatize quickly and deal with the issues of competition, regulation, loss of national wealth, growth of the economy, and unemployment, later. The question was when? It will be too late this "later." But, the IMF and EU focus only on macroeconomic issues, such as the size of the national debt and government's deficit (60% and 3% of the GDP) according to Maastricht criteria, even in the middle of a deep recession, than on structural issues, such as efficiency and competitiveness of the industry, selling the public enterprises at a correct market price[120], morality and work ethics, incentives, employment, and indigenous value system. These new private monopolies will be more efficient in production than the government, but they will be "more efficient" in exploiting their monopoly power, too; employees and consumers will suffer. Privatization has a drastic impact on employment and on national wealth and these are the major arguments against privatization and its enormous social cost.

Of course, there is some truth on this issue and from the other side; the low productivity of the public sector (which is very unethical from the side of employees). These unproductive employees cannot be promoted, their salaries should be low, and they might lose their jobs, too. Actually, the profit of this new private firm is going to come from trimming the payroll and eliminating the permanent jobs to its workers. Economists, as social scientists, have to focus on overall efficiency (the well-being for the entire society) and not on specific private firm's objective. There are enormous social costs associated

[120] Today, with this undervalued stock market, the sales of SOEs will be at an unfair low price, which does not benefit the government (less revenue) and hurts the citizens (less employment and income and high uncertainty). Then, the pressure from the Troika for privatization is very suspicious.

with unemployment[121] and security costs associated with the foreign ownership of these new private firms, for which these foreigners do not care because their objective is different than the government's one. "Privatization often destroys jobs rather than creating new ones"[122]. Privatization, outsourcing, the moving of firms in countries with lower cost of production, the common currency, the illegal migration (mostly young male Muslims)[123] and the austerities from the Troika are some causes of the debt crisis, which generated today's high unemployment and the loss of the national wealth and the sovereignty of Greece. Thus, the people have to say "NO" to these obstacles of their well-being and of their existence.

Furthermore, with this excessive privatization, there can be a large social cost of unemployment (especially with the socialist and communist parties that exist in Greece)[124], manifested by urban violence, increased crime, social and political unrest[125], reduction in wages, and employment of illegal immigrants because they are the only ones, who can accept a low pay job (reverse discrimination). Also, widespread anxiety exists even among workers, who have managed under pressure to keep their jobs, a broader sense of alienation floats in the air; additional financial burdens on family members, who manage to remain employed or receiving a low pension are appearing, the withdrawal of children from private schools because the parents cannot afford the high tuitions and the 23% of the VAT has arrived, and the tremendous financial distress and high probability of bankruptcy among households are, now, a fact. The cost of unemployment is huge for the unemployed person, his family, the

[121] Unemployment is the worst deficiency of capitalism, which offsets all its other benefits and makes it the dismal socio-economic system. People must have the basic right of a decent and permanent job in our faired democratic societies. Unfortunately, today, even in Academia 70% of the professors are contingent faculty with no job security, many of whom have only part-time work and no health benefits. See, Juan Gonzalez, "A Journalist's View of the Assault on Public Education," *Academe*, September-October 2015, 8-11.

[122] See, Stiglitz (2002, 57).

[123] A new Muslim immigrant (jihadist) beheaded a person in Sweden (TV News 8/11/2015); but, "Swedish government admits that you [its citizens] have no right to free speech in Sweden," as it happened in the entire West. See, https://themuslimissue. wordpress.com/2015/08/11/sweden-ikea-witness-asylum-seeker-had-cut-at-least-one-head-off-the-attack-was-a-terrorist-act/. Greece has received more than a million of these peculiar people and her security is in danger. The hope of Europeans is the Christian Russia, as we are hearing from people all over Europe because the West is in complete apostasy.

[124] Greece has been suffering for more than thirty years with the socialists in power because they are against Greece's value system and against the nation's welfare, due to their corruption and their control from the "New Age" advisers ("modernizers," ἐκσυγχρονιστάς).

[125] These acts were going on to every EU member-nation (Spain, Greece, Italy, Portugal, England, Belgium, France, etc.). See, http://alternativenewsreport.net/category/riots-civil-unrest-uk-europe/.

market, and the entire society, and definitely, cannot be covered with some insignificant unemployment insurance. Their children without the appropriate education would be future unemployed citizens, too. Many young people, mostly educated (scientists), are going to EU countries and to Australia, as new immigrants to find employment, which will affect negatively the development of the country. The social cost will be even higher when public enterprises will be sold to foreigners. Foreign owners feel only one obligation towards their shareholders (this is the only pressure from the market to maximize their market value by reducing labor cost) and less of an obligation towards the social policy of the host country (its social welfare). Their decisions are not based on patriotism or on any other social values; their "values" are greed, fear, corruption, exploitation, and other similar "great" values.

Every citizen in a country (not only in Greece) must concern about high rates of unemployment, even when he himself is not unemployed at the moment. High general unemployment (the worst deficiency of the free market system) reduces individual's well-being (utility) by increasing social cost on the rest of the population and decreasing the nation's welfare. A high rate of general unemployment has negative effects on the population as a whole because of social effects, like higher crime rates, the imposition of higher taxes on the remaining employed people to finance increased welfare spending and to reduce the deficit. Also, it increases the income inequality within the society, it affects people's well-being by reducing their sense of personal economic security, it depresses wages, it increases their actual or perceived risk of job loss and anticipated unemployment, it restricts consumers' and investors' confidence, and it reduces people's patriotism. Then, unemployment creates general negative externalities (even suicides) and externalities arising from changes in individuals' perceived economic risks. All these have a negative effect on the social welfare. The number one objective of public policy must be full employment ($u \cong 0$) and economic growth and not a budget surplus and sell-off of the public wealth in the middle of a deep recession.

Undoubtedly, it is important for Greece to increase productivity, efficiency, growth, employment, independence, and welfare, but if this can be done with gradual restructuring of state enterprises, there is no need for privatization. Public sector employment, especially of white-collar workers, was always excessive in Greece the last 30 years. But, moving people from low-productivity jobs in state enterprises to unemployment does not increase a country's income, growth, and it certainty does not increase the welfare of its citizens. The moral is simple in economics and in our lives: "Moderation is the best solution"[126]; and human beings are very complex entities (persons) and not only a primitive economic being. Thus, privatization needs to be part of a more comprehensive program and not because the suspicious IMF, the controlled ECB, and the distrustful EU say so, which entails creating jobs in tandem with the inevitable job destruction that privatization often entails; but, if there are national security issues and low market prices of the public assets, due to the financial crisis, privatization must be avoided, independently what the "experts," the "technocrats" or the "globalists" and all the other "illiterate wise" people are saying and the ignorant politicians are carrying it out. As many believe lately, globalization and technology have increased income inequality around the world[127] and have reduced the wages, salaries, and income and have increased unemployment in developed countries, so they might be able to compete with the developing ones. It is apparent to everyone that the performance of public enterprises had been far from satisfactory and they suffered sustained losses and were a major burden on the government budget, which is a serious ethical issue of our self-interest societies, today. But, the responsibility falls on the political parties and not on the Greek citizens.

PRIVATIZATION: A THEORITICAL AND GRAPHICAL PRESENTATION

The term "privatization" is over eighty years old. It had been introduced in 1930s and denotes the process of transferring ownership of state-owned enterprises (SOEs) from the public sector (governments) to the private sector

[126] But, the latest Greek politicians did not know the Greek language, history, culture and of course, they did not understand this Greek proverb (Πᾶν μέτρον ἄριστον). These puppet politicians destroyed the Greek paideia and are against Orthodoxy, which were the foundation of Hellenism. Now, the country and her citizens are in big trouble, due to the "imported" ignorance.

[127] This has been said by four Nobel Laureates (Robert Solow, Finn Kydland, George Akerlof, and Robert Fogel). See, *The Wall Street Journal*, August 25, 2008, pp. A1 and A2. Globalization has increased the correlation between economies ($\rho_{A,B} = +1$) and this has deteriorated the global portfolio diversification and investment (their risk cannot be minimized anymore). Then, even capitalists are worse-off with their imposition of globalization.

(businesses, MNCs). This can involve the denationalization[128] of this enterprise or industry as well as allowing the private sector to provide what had been considered government (public) services. Privatization, then, refers to transfer not only the assets (public wealth), but also any government function to the private sector, including governmental functions like, revenue collection, law enforcement, and others. Also, privatization has been used to describe the buyout of the majority or all shares of a public-owned corporation; privatizing its publicly traded stock. Investors, who will invest in these securities, will have an increase in their wealth and their utility, but the effect on social welfare is negative, especially with the forced privatizations by the Troika (the "Institutions," θεσμοί), where the future generations will lose their national wealth[129].

The expected objectives by the governments[130], the possible effects, and the social benefits (SB) of privatization can be the followings: efficiency, high productivity, higher production and more profitability for the private firm, higher tax revenue for the government, lower deficits, liquidity in capital markets, and more new innovations[131]. But, there is a tremendous social cost (SC) or losses accompanying all these outcomes; like, high unemployment, job uncertainty, minimum wages without health benefits, low personal income, national security issues, tax avoidance, evasion, and inversion by these private MNCs, loss of public wealth, dependency on foreign firms, capital, and markets, private monopolies, higher prices, social inequality, redistribution of

---

[128] Privatization (ἰδιωτικοποίησις) or denationalization (ἀποκρατικοποίησις), which considered by some Greek politicians a more "politically correct" term and a better one to be perceived by the people, are actually having the same meaning. Of course, the results are the same; the national wealth becomes private (business) and mostly foreign wealth, which its present value is determined by the financial markets. "Business is about maximizing profits. Big business has organized. This site is about their organizations: the International Monetary Fund (IMF), the World Trade Organization (WTO), and the World Bank (3 faces of the same hydra). Their philosophy and movement in this country is commonly called neoconservatism, in Europe and the rest of the world neoliberalism. They also go by the appellations of flat worlders, and globalizers. A more fitting label is robber barons. Through donations and their big stick the media they dominate American politics." See, http://www.skeptically.org/wto/. Now, they dominate the EU politics and have caused serious problems to the indebted nations. Greece is losing her entire public wealth, which is a plan of the Quartet (the "robber barons").

[129] From the ethical point of view, these forced privatizations (expropriations) of the national wealth of the future generations, who are not responsible for the current debts and the corrupted governments, are completely unethical actions and policies.

[130] Actually, the governments are against selling-off the public wealth at very low market prices; but, they have no choice, they have to obey to the lenders' claims. Indebted countries are truly under occupation by their greedy creditors.

[131] See also, Kallianiotis (2011c and 2012, 36-37).

income from domestic earners (government) to foreigners (MNCs), and loss of national sovereignty. The question is, here: Are the social benefits of privatization exceeding its social costs (SB > SC)? Unfortunately, the answer is NO! It is obvious by observing the reaction and opposition of all citizens, except of the international organizations and a few neo-liberal, neo-conservative bureaucrats or globalizers (New Age followers), who have some highly paid secured (at the moment) jobs and are ignorant of what is the ultimate social objective of a sovereign nation and its citizens (they ignore even their own long-term objective). Public sector employees and private ones differed fundamentally in their acceptance of risk and they were exposed dissimilarly to economic shocks. Public sector employees enjoyed extended dismissal protection and worked in enterprises that very rarely went bankrupt, before the taking over of countries by the Troika (or "Institutions," as a more politically correct term) or other globalist agents. Thus, these workers faced a reduced risk of losing their jobs, in comparison with employees in the private sector. For this reason, their compensation was lower than those, who work in private businesses. Unfortunately, lately, public and private sector employees in Euro-zone nations and mostly, in Greece are all in big trouble because the nations lost their sovereignty and are controlled by the Troika that is against any labor's rights.

The evaluation of privatization must be from the point of view of the society's well-being and not from the profit maximization one of multinational firms. Every policy or economic decision must have the same objective, which is the public interest. The total welfare of a country (given the factor endowments and the state of the economy) must be improved continuously. General concerns about the political system, the expected state of the economy or anxiety about crime rate or high risk or job losses are affecting negatively the social welfare. Also, the measurement of social welfare (SW) requires some ethical, moral, and country-specific standards (indigenous value system), which involve internal and eternal value judgments. For this reason, we cannot generalize the solution for all the different nations that are facing privatization. Of course, as a welfare criterion can be the growth of the wealth of the society (nation's GNP), which increases employment ($u \cong 0$) and production (keeping prices stable, $\pi \cong 0$). This implies that the income distribution will be ethical and just (not exactly equal)[132]. A high (out of control) growth can lead to reduction in social welfare, due to waste, pollution, huge fluctuations of

[132] An equal income distribution may induce some very productive individuals to work less (lack of incentives); thus, leading to a reduction of GNP and social welfare.

business cycles, creation of bubbles, irrational euphoria, high debts, and negative mental, physical, and spiritual (except if they have a strong faith) effects on humans. Efficiency (saving of recourses) is very important in social welfare maximization (requires respect of the creation and individuals). Financial markets stability (normal return and low risk) is necessary to attract long-term investments and prevent speculators and opportunists through regulation and to improve the wealth of the investors and their utility. We cannot accept an action, which increases some individuals' utilities, but one individual's utility is decreasing because all humans are equal (have the same "worthiness"). The criterion must be objectively measured and a Pareto-Optimal one[133].

A graphical solution of the privatization is presented in Figure 1. The optimal level of privatization of SOEs is where the SW is maximized [max $SW = SB - SC$]. This point is where the marginal benefits of privatization (MB_P), due to increase in efficiency, productivity, government revenue, increase in capital market liquidity, reduction in national debt, etc. are offset by the marginal cost of socio-economic distress (MC_{SED}), due to increase in unemployment, reduction in public wealth, increase in dependency, creation of private monopolies, increase in prices, increase in risk, negative effect on the security of the country, etc. Figure 1 shows that at zero (0) [$\%PO(PP)$][134] ratio, the country has only SOEs, which provide high SB, but they also have a relatively high SC. At 100% [$\%PO(PP)$] ratio, the SOEs are zero (0), we have only POEs, where the SC is huge and exceeds the SB (SC > SB). The optimal level of privatization is at point B (point of bliss), where the SW is maximized; the condition is: $MB_P = MC_{SED}$ (the marginal benefits of privatization are equal to the marginal cost of socio-economic distress). The objective of a government must be to privatize as many SOEs as they are needed; but, the proportion of privatization must be below 50% at the optimal ratio (PP^*). After this point, the SW is falling and it is becoming negative after 75% of private ownership.

The social welfare (perfection) function can be written as follows:

[133] According to Pareto-optimal criterion any change in our socio-economic system that makes at least one individual better-off and no one worse-off is an improvement in the social welfare. Austerities have made millions of people worse-off; then, these policies are imperfect (wrong) because deteriorate the social welfare.

[134] Where, $\%PO$ = percentage of private ownership, PP = proportion of privatization, SW = social welfare, SB = social benefits, SC = social costs, $SOEs$ = state-owned enterprises, and $POEs$ = private-owned enterprises.

$$\text{Optimize} \quad \begin{array}{l} SW = SB - SC = f(u^A, u^B, u^C, \ldots, u^N) \\ f_{u^A} > 0, \ldots f_{u^N} > 0 \end{array} \tag{1}$$

Subject to: tastes, employment, socio-economic benefits, investments in Treasuries, unemployment, disinvestments, investments in private securities[135], endowments, technology, revenue[136], and indigenous value system.

The social benefits can be presented as follows,

$$\begin{array}{l} SB_t = f(E_t, HE_t, JS_t, \overline{P}_t, NW_t, IG_t, Y_t, \overline{\sigma}_t, S_t \,\&\, S_t, R\&D_t, SMI_t, NI_t, \phi_t, IVS_t) \\ f_E > 0, f_{HE} > 0, f_{JS} > 0, f_P < 0, f_{NW} > 0, f_{IG} > 0, f_Y > 0, f_\sigma < 0, f_{S\&S} > 0, f_{R\&D} > 0, \\ f_{SMI} > 0, f_{NI} > 0, f_\phi > 0, f_{IVS} > 0 \end{array} \tag{2}$$

and the social cost function can be as,

$$\begin{array}{l} SC_t = f(u_t, I_t, JU_t, LP_t, \overline{w}_t, PM_t, Q_t, S_t, TA_t, BD_t, NW_t, SU_t, LG_t, LNS_t, PP_t, BOC_t) \\ f_u > 0, f_I > 0, f_{JU} > 0, f_{LP} < 0, f_{\overline{w}} < 0, f_{PM} > 0, f_Q < 0, f_S > 0, f_{TA} > 0, f_{BD} > 0, f_{NW} < 0, \\ f_{SU} < 0, f_{LG} > 0, f_{LNS} > 0, f_{PP} > 0, f_{BOC} > 0 \end{array} \tag{3}$$

where, SW = social welfare (perfection), $u^A, u^B, u^C, \ldots, u^N =$ utility (happiness, prosperity, blissfulness, perfection) of individuals A, B, C, …, and N in the nation, SB = social benefits, SC = social cost, SOE = state-owned enterprises, POE = private-owned enterprises, E = efficiency, HE = high employment, JS = job security, $\overline{P}$ = low prices, NW = big national (public) wealth, IG = independence of government, Y = high income, $\overline{\sigma}$ = low risk, S&S = security and safety, R&D = research and development, SMI = stock market index, NI = new innovations, ϕ = stability, IVS = indigenous value system, u = unemployment, I = inefficiency, JU = job uncertainty, LP = low productivity, $\overline{w}$ = minimum wages, PM = private monopolies, Q = low production (output), S = government subsidies, TA = tax avoidance, BD = budget deficits, SU = strong unions, LG = large governments, LNS = loss of national sovereignty, PP = proportion of privatization, BOC = bailout cost, $E(R_P^G)$ = expected return of a portfolio in government securities, $\sigma_{R_P}^G$ = risk

[135] $E(R_S^G) < E(R_S^{PF})$ and $\sigma_{R_S}^G < \sigma_{R_S}^{PF}$ $\Rightarrow$ cost of capital and risk are increasing with privatization.

[136] Where, $CIF^G = COF^{PF}$ and $R^G < R^{PF}$ (G = government and PF = private firms).

of a portfolio in government securities (interest rate risk or maturity risk)[137], $E(R_P^{PF})$ = expected return of a portfolio in private securities, $\sigma_{R_P}^{PF}$ = risk of a portfolio in private securities, K = capital[138], L = labor[139], i_{t+1} = interest rate next period, w_{t+1} = wages next period, R = revenue, G = government, and PF = private firm.

The optimality conditions for the maximization of social welfare are: (1) Efficient consumption; (2) Efficient production; (3) Efficient product-mix; (4) Democracy; (5) Optimal investment; (6) Social justice; (7) Social (national) wealth[140]; (8) Self-sufficiency; (9) Independence; (10) National currency; (11) Domestic public policies; (12) Indigenous value system; (13) Fair distribution of wealth; (14) Homogeneity of population; and (15) Sovereignty. The above social welfare function [equation (1)] must rise and this can happen only with individuals' happiness (utility). But, after a point, where the SC is increasing drastically, compared to the SB, the SW is falling (Figure 1). Our objective for this privatization is to reach a position, where we will make all individuals in the country happier (εὐημεροῦντας), without making anyone less happy. This only will be an efficient social state[141]. An appropriate factor ownership is necessary for any sovereign nation by keeping the SC at a minimum. The distribution of factor ownership must be such that each citizen, who is risk-averse, can buy the consumption bundle (and has the satisfaction that his country maximizes national wealth) with the income that his factor ownership generate to him not only enough disposable income for consumption, but he has some savings (that will be invested) with a savings rate that exceeds the inflation rate[142] and he lives in an environment that social and economic

[137] Lately, a default risk appeared for government securities, too. Even, the U.S. government securities are not risk-free anymore, after the latest "planned" financial crisis and their downgrading by *Standard and Poor's* in August 2011. Also, currency (cash money) is not risk-free because there is inflation and currency depreciation that reduce its value. Even gold has a high volatility in its price (risk). With our retreats from any human values, we have created a very uncertain world. Where are we going? Do we know what are we doing? Do our leaders understand where are they leading their people? Do we know what the objective in life is?

[138] Assumed that $K^{SOE} < K^{POE}$. Then, $K_{t+1} \uparrow \;\Rightarrow\; i_{t+1} \uparrow$ (with the privatization).

[139] Assumed that $L^{SOE} > L^{POE}$. Then, $L_{t+1} \downarrow \Rightarrow w_{t+1} \downarrow \Rightarrow u \uparrow$ (after privatization).

[140] See, Kallianiotis (2011c).

[141] From the continuous demonstrations all over Europe, we can see that the current privatizations are making many individuals unhappy. Then, EU (Troika's) social state is not efficient. The PP ratio exceeds the optimal ratio (PP*). Then, the leaders of the countries are responsible for pursuing these inefficient policies. Voters are not excused from their responsibility, too.

[142] See, Kallianiotis (2015b).

distress are at a very low level, which corresponds to the welfare-maximizing configuration of the national economy. Of course, low taxes, due to government efficiency and fair distribution of tax obligation to every physical and legal person (businesses)[143]; and zero property taxes at least, on the first home (only income taxes) are necessary[144], but not sufficient conditions for social welfare maximization.

Undoubtedly, incentives are necessary for the public enterprises; but an uncorrupted, efficient, and acting in favor of the country government is imperative[145]. Rewards to people, who work (have high productivity) and the opposite for the others are important. A wage differential must exist to public firms, too, but not a discrepancy of hundreds of millions of dollars, as it happen to the unfair private firms[146], with their enormous executive payments and minimum wages without health benefits for the workers. This will ensure reasonable utilization of labor and increase in productivity and efficiency. Public employees must be socially responsible and maintain a social discipline with education and continuous attempt for moral and ethical uplift. If state-owned enterprises make people feel happier, with the same consumption bundle and income, it is, other things being equal, preferable and promotes national security, self-sufficiency, independence, job security, sovereignty, and social welfare. People working in the public sector were affected less strongly by general economic shocks than were people working in the private sector and their well-being were less sensitive to fluctuations in unemployment rates[147]. Of course, the public sector attracts more risk-averse individuals than

---

[143] The problem in the US and EU is that businesses do not pay taxes and governments cannot impose taxes on them *(sic)*. See Kallianiotis (2011b).

[144] All sources of incomes must have a fair tax (progressive), but a home cannot be taxed. Property taxes (rent on your own home) are completely unfair and unethical (capitalism is against property ownership, too).

[145] Unfortunately, corruption in Europe is high as it is all over the world (i.e., Siemens, VW, armaments, etc.). Greece had, the last 40 years, the most corrupted governments in her 7,000 years old history, the socialists of PASOK, the centrists of N.D., and some others that led the country to a new German "occupation" with three inhumane memoranda. A Greek ΣΔΟΥ (IRS) labor union official said that they do not collect taxes from wealthy individuals and big businesses; the SYRIZA government knows this and it cannot do anything because the Troika (through the memoranda) encourages their tax-evasion. Are they New Age policies? (TV News *MEGA* October 7, 2015).

[146] See, Kallianiotis (2011b).

[147] This changed during the recent debt crisis and the dependence of nations on loans from the anti-social IMF and the Troika. Public employees lost all their privileges that the previous sovereign European nations had offered to them. Nations cannot pursue their own public policies anymore. This is the beginning of the social dissolution of the nation; the first stage of globalization. Then, imagine what will be its second and third stage! The trend has been traced out and the Euro-zone member-nations are on a steep cliff.

does the private sector and for this reason salaries are lower. With a relatively large and efficient public sector, the country's risk was lower and the social welfare was higher. With respect to productivity, responsible were the government officials, who supervised the public sector. People must learn from kindergarten to be conscientious and to respect themselves and to be fond of their country[148].

Unfortunately, economic liberals (pseudo-conservatives) claim that society is better off when allocation is done by the "dirty" speculators in the unregulated "free-markets," rather than by the exercise of a mixed power (political, social, economic, ethical, cultural, traditional, spiritual, and others) to all citizens and markets. The negative results of globalization are already obvious from now to the entire world. Sovereign nations must undertake actions, which can be justified either on efficiency grounds, on equity grounds, on historical realities, and on cultural peculiarities[149], if the "dark powers" allow it to happen. The personal utilities (the struggle to reach perfection) of the citizens are interdependent and the social welfare function incorporates an ethical valuation of all citizens' individual utility functions, for this reason homogeneity[150] plays a major role in nations' continuity and well-being (the illegal immigration and all the other refugees that the Middle East crisis[151] brought to Europe and mostly, in Greece have changed her identity and objectives). Leaders, economists, and scientists in general are responsible to determine the welfare-maximizing state (the "point of bliss," the state of perfection) for the entire society. We cannot provoke or scandalize or underrate any person in our society. Political leaders must refurbish their old

---

[148] And of course, "the beginning of the wisdom is the fear of God."

[149] Greece, for example, with her 7,000 years old Hellenic culture and her 2,000 years old Orthodoxy cannot follow what the others are doing. The other sub-cultures have to follow, if they want to benefit, from the unique Hellenic-Orthodox civilization and paideia. The world leaders must understand this basic historic and true knowledge. We in academia cannot compromise with any inferior values; either with the current sub-culture of waste (capitalism) or the previous sub-culture of oppression (communism). These are two extreme philosophical systems, which are completely imperfect and rejectable. See, Kallianiotis (2014b).

[150] <<Ὅμαιμον, ὁμοεθνές, ὁμόγλωσσον, ὁμόθρησκον καί ὁμότροπον>> are necessary characteristics of all people of a nation, according to Herodotus (Ἡρόδοτος; 5th century B.C.). Otherwise, this is not a nation, but a mixture of different people trying to maximize their self-interest by biting and cheating the "system."

[151] This enormous humanitarian crisis cannot has been done by mistake; it is a well-planned action against Christians in Middle East and of course, against the Christian Europe. Russia, as a Christian Orthodox nation, has perceived it. For this reason the controlled media are against Russia's involvement in this crisis to protect the Christians.

power[152], otherwise, citizens will lose their conquests after so many centuries of struggles and fights.

Of course, the objective function of a public enterprise is completely different from that of a private firm. Thus, the main effect of privatization is the drastic change of the objective function of the SOE (public firm), when it is privatized and causes serious social disturbances. Public enterprises' objective is social prosperity:

$$\begin{aligned} \max \quad & SP_t = f(E_t, HE_t, PE_t, LS_t, Q_t, S_t, \overline{P}_t, \overline{R}_t, NW_t, PM_t, \iota_t, S\&S_t, \phi_t) \\ & f_E > 0, f_{HE} > 0, f_{PE} > 0, f_{LS} > 0, f_Q > 0, f_S > 0, f_P < 0, f_R > 0, f_{NW} > 0, \\ & f_{PM} < 0, f_\iota > 0, f_{S\&S} > 0, f_\phi > 0 \end{aligned} \tag{4}$$

where, SP_t = social prosperity, E_t = efficiency, HE_t = high employment, PE_t = permanency of employment, LS_t = lump sum payment at retirement (*efapax*), Q_t = output, S_t = subsidies, $\overline{P}_t$ = low prices, $\overline{R}_t$ = decent revenue for the government, NW_t = national wealth, PM_t = private monopolies, ι_t = equality among citizens, $S\&S_t$ = security and safety, and ϕ_t = a stability of the democratic nation factor.

Public enterprises are more concerned about employment, which increases social welfare of the country. Then, the objective function of a publicly owned enterprise is more complex and broader [equation (4)]. We assume that public firms are concerned, first, about employment and the social prosperity of all citizens; second, about revenue for the government; thirdly, about the preservation of the national wealth and protection of the citizens from the private monopolies. The standard explanation for the public sector's concern for employment can be a "welfarist"[153] one (the public sector seeks to maximize social prosperity and social benefits, and consequently, social welfare).

[152] Unfortunately, today, political leaders have zero power. They are completely controlled by many different powers and by businesses (διαπλοκή), which finance their very expensive political campaigns. Then, democracy is in crisis!..

[153] See, Bhaskar and Khan (1995, 270).

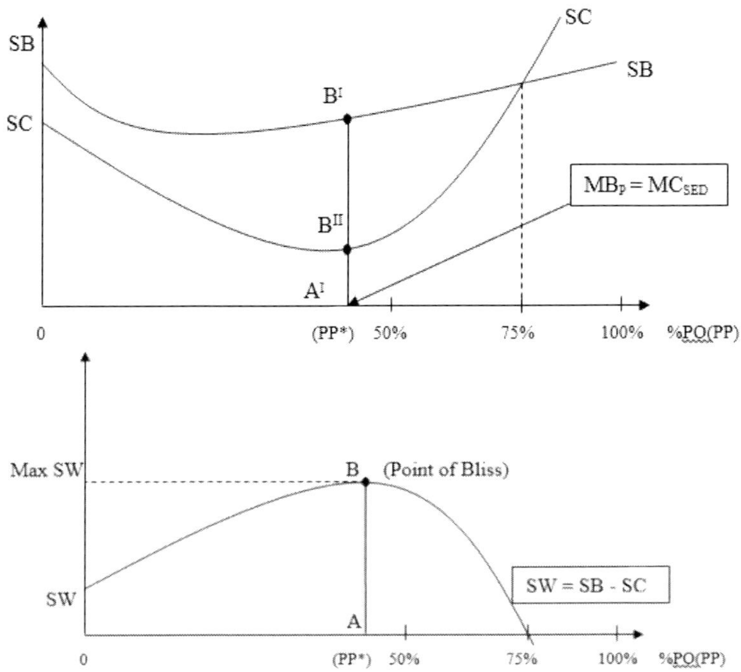

Note: SW = social welfare (perfection), SB = social benefits, SC = social cost, and $(SW = SB - SC)$, $\%PO$ or PP = percentage of private ownership or proportion of privatization, PP^* = the optimal level of privatization in the country, where the SW is maximized. T = taxes, MB_P = marginal benefits of privatization, MC_{SED} = marginal cost of socio-economic distress. The condition of optimization is: $MB_P = MC_{SED}$. To the left of this point (A) the SBs are high because of high employment, job security, low prices, big national (public) wealth, independence of government, high income, low risk, security and safety, and stability. Also, the SC is high because of inefficiency, low productivity, low production, subsidies, budget deficits, strong unions, and large governments. To the right of this optimal ratio (PP^*), the SBs are high, due to efficiency of the private firms, higher productivity, more output, high profitability, higher revenue for the governments (T), lower deficits, increase in government spending, liquidity in capital markets, and innovations. But, the SC is high, too, because unemployment is high, reduction in public wealth, dependency on foreign capital and markets, private monopolists, higher prices, high risk, high bail out cost, social inequality, redistribution of income (from domestic earners to foreigners), reduction of country's security, and loss of sovereignty.

Figure 1. Graphical Solution of Privatization.

With widespread prevalence of unemployment in EU, after its integration and the uncontrolled inflows of illegal immigrants[154], a welfare-maximizing public-sector should push employment beyond the point, where the marginal cost equals marginal revenue. For this reason, output in public firms would also be greater than in private ones ($Q_t^G > Q_t^{PF}$) and prices lower than in private firms ($P_t^G < P_t^{PF}$). Further, excessive public sector employment could arise for another reason. The public sector might be used by politicians in order to create jobs in response to political pressure. This phenomenon is well spread in Greece and all over Europe and is called "clientelism" (πελατειασμός). Also, public enterprises in Greece were used by politicians (PASOK and N.D. parties) to employ their voters and their family members; then, the reason was "canvassing" (ψηφοθηρία), which is unethical and unfair for the rest of the citizens. Finally, another explanation can be "sociological" and complementary to the clientelist and canvassing explanations, which is also political. This is a motivation of public sector managers in the determination of a pattern of excess employment. These managers create jobs for those to whom they are tied by kinship or social bonds[155]. The permanency of employees without any evaluation for their performance was reducing public enterprises' productivity and augmenting labor cost (increase in budget deficits). Public employees, when they were retiring, they were receiving a significant lump sum payment (called *efapax*). Of course, some of the above practices caused serious inefficiency and high debt problems to Greece. Efficiency is necessary to all SOEs to increase social prosperity.

On the contrary, private firms (POEs) are concerned only about their profits:

$$\begin{aligned} \max \quad & \pi_t = f(R_t, \bar{\xi}_t, \bar{w}_t, i_t, \bar{T}_t, \varphi_t, d_t, BE_t, PM_t, \sigma_t^2) \\ & f_R > 0, f_\xi < 0, f_w < 0, f_i < 0, f_T < 0, f_\varphi > 0, f_d > 0, f_{BE} < 0, f_{PM} > 0, f_{\sigma^2} < 0 \end{aligned} \tag{5}$$

[154] Illegal migration is the number one problem in Greece and in the entire Europe the last twenty years. Those illegal immigrants are mostly Muslims and are driven forward to Greece by Turkish smugglers and are restricted by the Merkel plan in Greece, which is the objective of a Muslim Turkish policy and the anti-Greek EU (German) policy to dilute the Greek Orthodox-Christian identity. This is actually a dirty war, which is continued since the 12th century and European politicians are blissfully sleeping or they are responsible for these crises in the Middle East. This is a planned war against Christianity with all these jihadists in Middle East that are becoming refugees, lately. Of course, there are and a few Syrian Christians that left their homeland to be saved from the knifes of the ISIS. The hope of these Christians is the Orthodox Russia (TV News *MEGA* and *ALPHA*, October 26, 2015).

[155] See, Kallianiotis (2009, 75-76).

where, π_t = profit [or max $V = D + E$ = the market value of liabilities (D) and equity (E)], R_t = revenue ($P_t^{PF} . Q_t^{PF}$), $\overline{\xi}_t$ = executives' compensation, $\overline{w}_t$ = low real wage[156], i_t = cost of capital[157], $\overline{T}_t$ = lowest taxes, φ_t = a firm specific effect, d_t = deregulations, BE_t = business ethics, PM_t = private monopoly, and σ_t^2 = a risk factor.

Private businesses are producing where marginal cost equals to marginal revenue ($MC_t = MR_t$); actually, the private giant multinational firm is becoming a monopolist, with the lowest output and higher prices compared to the public one based on equation (5). Their first concern is the reduction of the labor cost, the increase in earnings by engaging in risky investment, the determination of CEOs' outrageous pay by themselves, and the maximization of the market price of their stocks by using a variety of "tricks." The tax avoidance, tax evasion, and tax inversion is the most common practice of businesses, which contribute to the high debts of governments. For these reasons privatization has a large negative effect on white-collar employment, clerical as well as managerial because they have high wages and with their outsourcing they cause unemployment domestically and avoid taxes legally. Private firms are very happy with all these deregulations since 1980 and they try to avoid business ethics, too, because they increase their cost and decrease competitiveness and profitability. Liquidity in financial market will increase together with the inequality in salaries between the executives (counting in hundreds of millions per annum) and the other employees (a few thousands per annum) and also no improvement in government revenue. These discrepancies are completely unethical, unfair, not patriotic, and waste of resources, without any positive effect on social welfare.

Furthermore, Aristotle's[158] social welfare plan had some secondary goals that served the ultimate goal[159]. They were the stability of the democratic state (that we do, today, through enforcement, police, secret services, spying, and terrorizing the citizens)[160] and the fulfillment of the state's ends, liberty and

[156] Firms (central banks, too) like inflation because their real cost is falling and they cause inflation by increasing the prices of their products and services (cost-push or supply-side inflation).

[157] What is completely unfair and unethical is that a large proportion of the cost of debt is paid (subsidized) by the poor taxpayers [$i_d(1-T)$ = cost of debt after tax].

[158] See, Kallianiotis (2014b).

[159] See, Drogalis (2008).

[160] Europe and the West have laws that prohibit even the freedom of speech. Greece was pressed to pass this law in September 2014. See, http://yiorgosthalassis.blogspot.com/2013/05/blog-

equality. Also, Aristotle's land distribution plan brought about a kind of parity between the rich and the poor. There is no excuse for Greece to ignore the wisdom of her forefathers. Today, the chasm between these two groups is widening and the middle-class is in extinction (wiping out)[161]. With the disappearance of the middle class, the upper class will fall from its "height" because it is relying on the previous one. The government should partially (less than 50%) privatize only its most inefficient, heavily subsidized, and those that are not part of the national security of the country firms and also, the least likely to upset political and social interest groups, ones. The nation must have high cohesion, solidarity, and patriotism among all stakeholders and preserve these values for the benefits of all citizens and for its national defense, especially today, with all these external pressures, internal Trojan horses (ἐθνομηδενισταί καί πατριδοκτόνοι), and its surrounding only by enemies. Of course, to maintain SOEs ownership in domestic private hands, it will be preferable relative to sell them to foreign bidders (alienation of public wealth), to find only domestic buyers and to sell these public firms to a satisfactory market price.

Political Considerations to Prevent Future Crises and Expropriations of National Wealths

A financial panic and a new global crisis in the next few years is very probable; this can be caused by the rating firms, by the central banks' policies, by the international institutions, by derivatives exposure and bank

post_7273.html. Also, I. N. Kallianiotis, *Christian Vivliografia*, August 27, 2014, 1-2. https://christianvivliografia.wordpress.com/2014/08/27/%CF%84%E1%BD%B8-%CF%84%CE%AD%CE%BB%CE%BF%CF%82-%CF%84%E1%BF%86%CF%82-%CE%B4%CE%BF%CF%85%CE%BB%CE%B5%CE%AF%CE%B1%CF%82-%E1%BC%90%CE%BD-%E1%BC%90%CE%BB%CE%B5%CF%85%CE%B8%CE%B5%CF%81%CE%AF%E1%BE%B3/.

161 After twenty five centuries from Aristotle's moral and ethical philosophical teachings and twenty centuries since we have had the revealed truth, today's "democracies" are acting much worse than Hellas in her Golden Age and Roman Empire around the year 33 A.D. Aristotle (384-322 B.C.) was a great Greek philosopher from North Greece (Macedonia), who was a student of Plato (447-347 B.C.) and the teacher of Alexander the Great (356-323 B.C.). Plato was a student of Socrates (469-399 B.C.), the greatest philosopher of all times. See, "Poverty Threaten 21% of Greek Population," *Crete Gazette*. http://www.cretegazette.com/2007-11/greece-poverty. php and http://www.indexmundi.com/g/r.aspx?c=gr&v=69.

interconnectedness, by unsustainable deficits and debts, by continuing the anti-growth austerities, which may trigger a global liquidity crisis. But, there is no possibility that Greece's exit from Euro-zone could cause any global or European crisis; her economy is very small (2% of the Euro-zone) to affect the global equilibrium (stability). These people (in Europe and the US), which pretend that they worry and they care for Greece's exit from Euro-zone are lying because their objective is different; they want to terrorize the other nations that no one can leave and go against globalization. Social disorder is also very probable during a new global financial crisis because people have lost their patience and their hope to their governments. Social disorder involves riots, strikes, sabotage, dysfunctions and other violent acts. It is distinct from social protest because disorder involves illegality, violence, and property destruction; which will be very risky for countries that carrying of arms is free[162]. The new "constructed" Ukraine crisis in Europe, the continuation of the cold war, together with the continuing EU austerities and the wrong German and IMF policies, the Islamic State of Iraq and Syria (ISIS), the millions of illegal immigrants in Greece and Europe that the foreign policies of the West created, which will generate serious security problems in Greece and will alter the European identity; and also the pressure from the "allies"[163] give very bad signals for the entire world of what it is coming (they are bringing).

Past experience has shown that countries have to be independent democracies, self-sufficient (even exercising protectionism for their domestic industries), promoting first the primary sector (agriculture), second the secondary one (manufacture), and lastly the tertiary sector (services). An economy specializing only in services has no future. The country must produce more goods and services than are needed for domestic consumption and export the excess production. But, the persistence of the West on cold war has put embargos, which affect negatively the economies of the small European nations. A nation has to have a decent growth and zero

---

[162] For example, see, http://www.theguardian.com/us-news/2015/oct/01/oregon-umpqua-community-college-shooting.

[163] See, "US, Israel Escalate Iran Spat," *The Wall Street Journal*, February 26, 2015, pp. A1and A11. EU voted on September 22, 2015 to distribute 120,000 asylum seekers among member-nations, but Czech Republic, Hungary, Romania, and Slovakia voted against this distribution plan. See, *The New York Times*, September 23, 2015, pp. A1 and A8. Also, Austria is putting a fence at its borders to keep immigrants out of the country. The continued Israel-Palestine conflict is a serious problem for the Middle East peace. See, http://www.democracynow.org/2015/10/19/ as_israel_ palestine_toll_mounts_an. An EU (Angela Merkel) plan forced Greece to keep 50,000 immigrants in Greece (TV News *MEGA* and *ALPHA*, October 26, 2015).

unemployment, also, it has to have a high saving rate (25% of the disposable income), a decent (above inflation) deposit rate, and a low debt. The financial markets and the entire economy have to be controlled (regulated) and every firm must comply with the socially imposed constraints. The ultimate objective of a country is maximization of its social welfare (minimization of the loss to society). We need a worldwide governmental intervention to support and regulate the national banking systems that are leading the nations to bankruptcies with their risky transactions and the need to be bailout during crises.

Also, central banks have to be public, supporting the public policies of the nation and not only the financial markets and institutions. A common central bank, like the ECB in Euro-zone, is the worst structure for the Europeans. Domestic public policies must deal with human beings, their welfare, and not how to dispose the public wealth and bail out the corrupted banks. Economic policies must have one objective; the prevention of future crises, as the one that the world and the EU experienced lately and is still going on. The Theory of Finance has to change from now; the government securities are not risk-free anymore because governments are controlled by the markets (Mammon). Who gave this power to the rating firms to overturn (even though that we know it is wrong) our global financial system? The negative effects of a financial crisis on the real economy and on peoples' lives are enormous. These existing financial markets, institutions, and policies have to be controlled by the governments of the sovereign nations; otherwise, they will generate very soon a global collapse and the worst civil unrest and destruction of the entire world, except if this is the objective of the uncontrolled "planners."

Central banks actually can monetize any amount of debt their governments issue, up to the point of a collapse of confidence in the country's currency. But, lately, some central banks around the world started selling US government securities (they sold $123 billion out of their $12.8 trillion holdings of US Treasuries), which can affect negatively the US economy[164]. If national income can pay the interest on the debt, with enough left over to reduce total debt as a percentage of GDP, then the situation should remain stable. If there is not enough national income left over after the interest to reduce the debt as a percentage of GDP, and if this condition persists, then the country will eventually go bankrupt. The same holds for all the EU member-nations; but, in trouble are those that are members of the EMU because they

[164] The sales were by China, Russia, Brazil, and Taiwan. See, *The Wall Street Journal*, October 8, 2015, pp. A1, A14, and C3.

have no independent central bank, no domestic currency, and no monetary policy to monetize the debts of their governments or to cause inflation. The deficits are sustainable only when,

$$(\dot{q}+\pi)-i>\left|\dot{t}-\dot{g}\right| \quad (6)$$

$$(5\%+2\%)-2\%>3\%$$

where, $\dot{q}$ = the growth of real output (GDP), π = inflation, $\dot{q}+\pi=\dot{y}$ = the growth of nominal GDP, i = borrowing (interest) cost (as a percentage of GDP), $\dot{t}$ = taxes, $\dot{g}$ = government spending, and $\dot{t}-\dot{g}<0$ = primary deficit (as a percentage of GDP).

The deficit is not sustainable if the inequality above is the opposite (<)[165]. This second case reveals the trend toward unsustainability, which encourages the sell-off of public wealth and makes the indebted nations worse than before. These debts (especially Greece's) should be forgiven, as it happened with the German debt in 1953[166]. The key factors in primary deficit sustainability (PDS) are borrowing costs (I), real output (Q), inflation (π), taxes (T), and government spending (G). The best way to move toward sustainability is to increase real growth (the production of the nation). Another way is the one that (the Troika)[167] EU is using for its member-nations, improving debt

165 Even in the US, the situation at the end of 2014 was: $(2.4\%+0.67\%)-2.65\%<2.97\% \Rightarrow 0.42\%<2.97\%$ = primary deficit, which shows it is Unsustainable. See, http://sub1.economagic.com/popular.htm. In EU, it was in 2014: $(1.3\%+0.6\%)-1\%<2.9\% \Rightarrow 0.9\%<2.9\%$ (assuming $i=1\%$ of the GDP), unsustainable, too. In Greece for 2013, it was: $(-3.9\%-0.9\%)-2\%<0.8\% \Rightarrow -3.9\%<0.8\%$ = primary surplus (*sic*), due to austerities, which is disastrous and inhumane. See also, https://www.imf.org/external/pubs/ft/scr/2014/cr14151.pdf. Also, https://www.treasurydirect.gov/govt/reports/ir/ir_expense.htm. Further, http://www.wsj.com/ articles/u-s-budget-deficit-in-2014-narrows-to-lowest-level-in-six-years-1413385493.

166 There is a parable in The Bible for debt forgiveness that resemble the case of German and Greek debts. "…the master forgave to his servant ten thousand talents (60,000,000 Drs or \$141,787,200), ... but that servant (Germany) laid hands on his fellow servant (Greece), who owed him a hundred denarii (74.78 Drs or \$176.714) and took him by the throat, saying, 'pay me what you owe!'… and the master said, 'should you not also have had compassion on your fellow servant, just as I had pity on you?" (Matthew 18:23-34). The calculations are from Kallianiotis (2015a). See also, http://www.debatingeurope.eu/2015/03/18/parallels-greece-today-german-debt-relief-1953/#.ViFDPk2FOM9.

167 The Troika is humiliating Greece for many years. Greece cannot accept any demands for deeper austerity, which is anti-growth and the country cannot pay the debt. Since August 2014, Greece has not taken any money from the Troika. On June 30, 2015, Greece had to

sustainability by increasing taxes, which is absolutely wrong during periods of recessions or depressions. Also, if taxes are held steady and spending is cut, the primary deficit shrinks, but this policy is contractionary and does not stimulate an economy that is in recession. The central banks' policies can affect inflation (π) and interest rate (I) cost of borrowing, which can affect the PDS and finally, the debt as a percentage of the GDP. In the absence of higher real growth, either politicians must reduce deficits or the central banks must produce inflation and reduce the cost of borrowing, with their excess supply of liquidity. But, for all these scenarios to work, the country must be independent, which means to stay out of the EMU. These politicians that forced the accession of their nations to Euro-zone, without a referendum, are responsible for these crises, due to loss of their public policies[168].

Data on public and private debt and deficits, on economic performance, on unemployment, and the buildup of derivatives inside megabanks are readily available, but conventional economic models and economists do not want to see the truth (sic); they follow this anti-scientific trend to destruction and they do not want to prevent the coming new global crisis, due to the American structural problems and the European ones that follow this neo-classical, neo-liberal, anti-social, New Age view. The real growth of the economy ($\dot{q}_t$) is measured as follows:

$$\dot{q}_t = \dot{y}_t - \pi_t \tag{7}$$

where, $\dot{q}_t$ = the growth of real GDP, $\dot{y}_t$ = the growth of the nominal GDP, and π_t = the inflation rate.

A nation can have a good real growth of 3% by having negative nominal growth (- 1%) and deflation (- 4%): $3\% = (-1\%) - (-4\%)$. This 3% real growth seems to be a desirable outcome, based on advances in technology and productivity, alternative sources of energy, embargos, and reduction in the

pay €1.5 billion to the IMF and on July 20, 2015, it had to pay €3.5 billion to redeem bonds held by the ECB. The first priority for Greece must be the salaries and pensions of its citizens and later with its growth, it can start paying foreigners. Of course, Greeks do not worry too much because they know: <<Ζητεῖτε δέ πρῶτον τήν βασιλείαν τοῦ Θεοῦ καί τήν δικαιοσύνην αὐτοῦ, καί ταῦτα πάντα προστεθήσεται ὑμῖν.>> (Ματθ. στ΄ 33). Now, after the elections of September 20, 2015 and the third memorandum, the country is worse than it was and the Troika (τριάς) has become Quartet (τετράς).

[168] The ex-Prime Minister of Greece (but not a Greek himself), Costas Semites, and many others from his government must be in jail for the harm that they did to this historic nation and its proud people.

price of oil, imports from China and other low cost of production and low quality countries, and more efficiency and price controls, can result in certain products dropping in price over time. Then, why deflation is bad? Deflation helps consumers and workers because it increases their purchasing power, but it hurts the Treasury and the banks [reduces the taxes and increases real rate of interest; equation (8)], and for this reason, it is firmly opposed by the central banks and of course by the ECB. Central banks prefer inflation because it erases government debt, reduces the debt to GDP ratio, props up the banks, can be taxed, and lowers the real cost of capital. Thus, central banks and the ECB are working for the banks, businesses, and their governments; their policies are against people's interest.

$$r_t = i_t - (-\pi_t) \tag{8}$$

where, r_t = the real rate of interest, i_t = the nominal rate of interest, and π_t = the inflation rate.

Consequently, central banks like inflation and this is their objective; thus, economic growth and employment are incidental by-products of the drive to inflation. ECB[169] likes its power and the control that exercises on the central banks of the Euro-zone member-nations. The free market economy needs inflation and the central banks cause it[170]. As long as deflation is a "threat," the central banks will continue with zero target rate, enormous money supply, and efforts to devaluate their currencies in order to import inflation through higher import prices. Real growth is more important than nominal growth, but it is being ignored by the controlled central banks. It seems that the Fed will pursue this easy money (quantitative easing), which started in December 2008, (printing money) policy (pseudo-remedy) as far as possible until global investors finally lose confidence in its currency (the US dollar) and in bonds denominated in dollars.[171] Countries need publicly-owned central banks so that bankers and financiers could not use the printing of money to control the

[169] The ECB gives funds to meet the needs of Greek banks through a program known as Emergency Liquidity Assistance (ELA). On June 17, 2015, the ECB raised the ceiling by €1.1 billion to €84.1 billion. The ECB is in control of the ELA. Since the beginning of July 2015, the ECB cut completely the liquidity for the Greek banks and closed them by imposing capital controls, after the Greek NO (that they did not want a third memorandum) on a referendum on July 5, 2015. Greece is under occupation!..

[170] The US Fed said that there is no Phillips curve (inflation is not negatively related with unemployment). Very suspicious view.

[171] Fed increased the target federal funds rate by 0.25% to 0.50% on December 15, 2015. See, http://www.federalreserve.gov/newsevents/press/monetary/20151216a.htm.

affairs of the nation[172]. The controlled by Germany ECB has eliminated the monetary policy from the member-nations. Then, these nations have no tools of improving their economies or to get rid of their current economic crises. The EMU has unfolded as the worst nightmare for the poor European nations that made the mistake or were forced to join this monster[173]. Countries need independent domestic mixed public policies (fiscal and monetary) to correct their business cycles.

This current enormous liquidity is money that sits in banks as excess reserves and does not produce inflation[174] and of course, does not participate in investments. Inflation appears only if consumers and businesses borrow and spend these reserves as printed money. Investment takes place if there is demand for goods and services. Also, the high unemployment and low or negative growth keep prices low because wages, salaries, and income are very low. European economies are still in recession and some in depression. The best solution, for the current debt crisis and the new ones that are planned, is

[172] As President Woodrow Wilson mentioned about the Fed in 1915. "However it has come about, it is more important still that the control of credit also has become dangerously centralized. It is the mere truth to say that the financial resources of the country are not at the command of those who do not submit to the direction and domination of small groups of capitalists who wish to keep the economic development of the country under their own eye and guidance. The great monopoly in this country is the monopoly of big credits. So long as that exists, our old variety and freedom and individual energy of development are out of the question. A great industrial nation is controlled by its system of credit. Our system of credit is privately concentrated. The growth of the nation, therefore, and all our activities are in the hands of a few men who, even if their action be honest and intended for the public interest, are necessarily concentrated upon the great undertakings in which their own money is involved and who necessarily, by very reason of their own limitations, chill and check and destroy genuine economic freedom. This is the greatest question of all, and to this statesmen must address themselves with an earnest determination to serve the long future and the true liberties of men. This money trust, or, as it should be more properly called, this credit trust, of which Congress has begun an investigation, is no myth; it is no imaginary thing. It is not an ordinary trust like another. It doesn't do business every day. It does business only when there is occasion to do business. You can sometimes do something large when it isn't watching, but when it is watching, you can't do much. And I have seen men squeezed by it; I have seen men who, as they themselves expressed it, were put 'out of business by Wall Street', because Wall Street found them inconvenient and didn't want their competition." See, https://en. wikiquote.org/wiki/Woodrow_Wilson.

[173] Mark A. Wynne (2015, 9) said: "I think it is fair to say that most North American economists (and good number of European economists as well) felt that the idea of such a diverse group of countries sharing a common currency was doomed to fail at some point because the countries in question did not constitute what economists refer to as an 'optimum currency area.'"

[174] The true inflation is much higher than the official inflation, which is measured by changes in the methodology. The US official inflation was (- 0.04%) and the true inflation rate was (7%) in September of 2015. See, http://www.shadowstats.com/. Also, http://www. shadowstats.com/alternate_data/inflation-charts.

people to leave the big cities and go back to their villages and country sites, where their parents or grandparents were living.

Furthermore, the government has to intervene in all sectors and through regulations and by using effective policies must make the market work more efficiently for the entire country. The social and economic policies must constrain the aggressive and unfair market behavior and produce socially acceptable results for all citizens. The markets and institutions have been created to contribute to people's well-being, otherwise, we do not need them. Governments must control effectively all the social interest firms and there are many activities that fall into the government domain ("public goods"). These activities must be: national defense, public safety, health care, public utilities (electricity, gas, water, telephone), public transportation (airlines, railways, subways, metros, buses, etc.), public parks, the survival of endangered species, postal services, agricultural banks, defense-related manufacturing, and certain strategic industries, economic infrastructure (electric power, water supply systems, sewage systems, telecommunications, rail lines, roads, tunnels, bridges, canals, seaports, airports and air traffic control system), some hospitals and almost all schools (from kindergarten to universities)[175], security services, and the criminal justice system.

Also, it is well known, historically, that public goods cannot be provided by the free market. The value of these goods is hard to identify and to allocate among beneficiaries, who will enjoy them and will share their cost[176] (through a fair and efficient tax system). The citizens need education, incentives, national conscience, social cohesion, public wealth, national currency, public policies, security, safety, resource users' fees, ownership rights, social prosperity, freedom, protection of indigenous values and traditions, and common paideia, which would make it clear in their own interests to maintain the resources on a sustainable basis and bequeath them, even improved, to their children (the future generations), which is a common tradition for Greeks and their culture. The market is weak to allocate costs and benefits; but, a fair, just, honest, impartial, lawful, truthful, uncorrupted, democratic, and objective government intervention must allocate costs and benefits of shared public goods effectively. As it was mentioned above, in the *Politics*, Aristotle urged

[175] Today, one very serious problem is the debt of the students. They graduate and have a $200,000 debt from their student loans. In the US, the student debt, reported in June 2014, was exceeded $1.2 trillion, with over 7 million debtors in default (*The Economist*). Also, http://www.usnews.com/news/articles/2015/06/08/heaviest-college-debt-burdens-fall-on-3-types-of-students. Further, http://www.cnbc.com/2015/06/15/.

[176] Unfortunately, there will be some free riders (underground economy, illegal immigrants, etc.), but we can find solutions there, too.

democratic states to pay attention to both the wealthy and the poor. Then, our nations, today, and especially the controlled by the Troika, Euro-zone member-nations, with its anti-social policies, cannot be democracies! These poor nations are German protectorates[177]. Aristotle warned that "poverty is the cause of the defects of democracy" (1320a 36-37). The current signs are proving this warning.

Lastly, privatization of industries with natural monopolies, such as a high-way[178], water supply, etc., could lead to abuse of monopoly power. Of course, improvement of efficiency is necessary and the government must be responsible to pursue this objective. Today, due to market-based solutions (resource allocation, economic growth, efficiency, increase in government revenue, technological changes, national debt, outsourcing, globalization, "internal devaluation," etc.), ownership has shifted towards the private one and unfortunately, at a dramatic speed, without taking into consideration the negative impact on the citizens, due to the high risk of the uncontrolled (deregulated) financial market, where the private sector has to comply to its orders and objectives. There are cases that private-sector activities can exist-alongside with the public ones and when there is a need to transfer some to the private sector, the government must continue to hold 51% of the equity and be in a position to control the firm[179]. The state ought to control a range of core economic activities that have strong public-good characteristics, which were mentioned above. The objective of businesses must be only one; the nation's social welfare because they are part of the nation, too. Governments have to increase productivity and efficiency of the public sector and keep the state-owned enterprises, which provide national security, safety, and other public services, as public ones. Even, nationalization has proved recently with the

---

[177] See, Kallianiotis (2015c).

[178] The privatization of high-ways in Greece has increased the payments for tolls enormously and people were demonstrating against these high prices and avoiding paying tolls by saying that roads are "free goods" (TV News *ERT*, *ALTER*, *ALPHA*, *ANTENNA*, February 16, 2011 and other different dates). Now, EU forces Greece to sell-off to a German (public) company 14 airports, which are on remote islands. This act is criminal and against the people of these islands. The private owner of these airports will not offer any services because the cost will exceed the benefits and the poor citizens of the islands will suffer. This is a serious national security issue for Greece with her number one enemy in the east of these small islands. See, http://www.dailymail.co.uk/news/article-3202393/Greek-Prime-Minister-reneges-pre-election-promise-not-privatise-indebted-country-s-infrastructure-selling-14-airports-German-company.html.

[179] The citizens of the country (as voters) have to control the government. A corrupted and acting against the country's and citizens' interest political party must not be elected again. The punishment has to be serious and permanent, which will make wise and prudent the other parties.

current financial crisis, which has been created by the uncontrolled private firms (financial institutions) that can improve stability, certainty, and preserve jobs[180].

Conclusion

All the EU economies have two major problems: overconsumption (underproduction, competition among members, waste of resources, and outsourcing) and lack of savings (dis-saving and borrowing or spendthrift)[181]. The Euro-zone economies have, except the above, three extra major problems: common currency, lack of domestic public policies, and loss of national sovereignty. These cause current account deficits, capital account surpluses, and interest rate to be high, which over-valuated the euro and affected negatively the financial markets, the national debt, the oil prices, the inflation, the competitiveness, the growth and employment, and the social welfare of the nations. We must learn that we cannot live beyond our means indefinitely. Actually, there is a vicious cycle in the economy, due to the wrong public policies. This latest crisis started with deregulations, integrations, globalization, enormous debts, corruptions, deterioration of human values, and with high energy prices; it continued with a deteriorating housing sector, it followed with an ill-functioning financial market (greed and fear), it reached a slowing consumer and business spending, and it ended to a severe recession (the first depression of the 21st century)[182], which became worse with the Troika's austerities (new suspicious anti-growth economic theory). These debts are unbearable for the poor citizens of the future and unsustainable for the nations of our falling world.

---

180 Central banks should be public (SOEs) because the printing of money and their monetary policy ought to be done only with people's welfare as the ultimate objective.

181 See Kallianiotis (2007a).

182 Greece has been destroyed with the €240 billion bailout loan from the Troika (ECB, European Commission, and IMF). The lenders are pressing Greece to slash public spending, lay off employees, privatize its ports and sell-off all the SOEs (national wealth, even its islands), to increase taxes and VAT, to have a budget surplus of over 1% of the GDP in the middle of a depression, and other anti-growth policies. These austerities have made the recession, depression and for the country to receive the new installments has to continue with new memorandum (three so far). The answer is only one and forever; NO and immediately, out from the destructive Euro-zone. But, the terrorizing propaganda from the agents of globalization changed the mind of Greeks and went back to their continuing submission. Greece is under an economic war by EU and it seems that it will not avoid the military one.

European industrial nations (Germany, France, England, and others) cannot create conflicts among nations (i.e., Imia in Greece) to sell their weapons by lending money to the poor nations to buy their military equipment and improve the manufacturing of the corrupted and unhesitating nation-producers and their economic growth, plus the bribery and crimes that they generate in different governments[183]. Germany alone has profited €100 billion by the Greek economic crisis1[184]. Without investments in sustainable developments, without increases in domestic productions and reductions in imports, every EU nation will lose the competitiveness race, as it has happened with the Euro-zone member-nations, due to the overvalued common currency. Even today (end of 2015), the EU economic data are very disappointing. The Euro-zone ones are catastrophic. The economies need a mixed expansionary economic policy (fiscal and monetary). The neo-liberal controlled EU policies are against this policy and people and nations are in devastation. Privatizing Europe cannot solve the European crises, but generates permanent crises, which will affect negatively all the future generations[185]. The global uncertainty, the deregulation of financial markets, the integration of unequal and different nations, the sell-offs of the SOEs, the private monopolists (no one respects the anti-trust laws anymore, even the courts)[186], the corruption in business and politics (corporations do not pay taxes)[187], the illegal migration[188], and the other domestic problems, due to globalization and

[183] These politicians and individuals, who are involved in these briberies and other illegal agreements must go to jail and their assets must be confiscated because they are responsible for the current debt crisis in Greece and in Europe.

[184] See, http://www.mirror.co.uk/news/world-news/germany-profited-100billion-euros-greek-6229502.

[185] See, https://www.tni.org/files/download/privatising_europe.pdf.

[186] The EU levied a record €1.06 billion ($1.56 billion) fine against Intel in May 2009, alleging the computer chip giant abused its dominant position in the microprocessor market (*The Wall Street Journal*, September 22, 2009, pp. A1, B1, and B6).

[187] Corporations and wealthy individuals paid no taxes. Companies have become all too astute at paying for loopholes, which allow them to shift profits abroad, or move their gains (on paper) to foreign low-tax/no-tax nations (in Switzerland, Luxemburg, and off-shore centers). Anyone who is serious about closing the budget deficits should consider the changes in what corporations pay in taxes, which will reduce the debts of the governments. The EU ordered Starbucks and Fiat Chrysler to pay back taxes (*The Wall Street Journal*, October 22, 2015, pp. A1 and B2).

[188] Greece has flooded with millions of illegal (Muslim) immigrants and refugees, which will cause serious safety and security problems for the Greek citizens. Greece as a Christian Orthodox nation, which has suffered by the Muslim invasions since the 7th century A.D. and its 400 years of occupation by these barbarians has to have zero acceptance policy for Muslims. The entire Europe has a very serious problem with all these millions of immigrants from Asia and Africa. This situation is a well-planned phenomenon to destroy

integration are going to change our economic system (many economic laws do not hold anymore and we have to bail out all these untrustworthy banks and other businesses). The only prediction that we can do for the future, after the current worst global recession[189] and the European debt crises and depressions, is that this new economic system, "globonomics," will be the last in our socio-economic history, except if we will decide to go back to a value oriented system.

These corrupted people in Brussels, in financial markets, and in institutions (the originators of the European crisis) need some knowledge in value-oriented welfare economics and business ethics. The current crisis was not an economic one, but a moral, ethical, social, spiritual, educational, and political crisis, which was expected by every prudent person after all these mistakes (liberalism) that were made since 1960s. But, loss of confidence in the EU, Euro-zone, and in the global financial system can rarely be restored[190]. Very likely, a new system will be needed, with a new humane foundation that can engender new confidence. This century can be called as the century of misinformation because the media are controlled and their "news" are just propaganda. We wait to see. We have to educate and awaken the citizens so they could become active citizens and go back to their indigenous traditional values, otherwise there will be no hope. Allowing the corrupted (puppet) politicians to sell Europe's soul would be the worst mistake in European history[191].

Happily, privatizations declined sharply in 2008, driven by the sharp fall in IPOs. The financial crisis reduced the market prices of the SOEs, which contributed to a decline of the private sector's demand, due to credit markets turmoil, too. But, the crisis itself has created pressure for privatization by the lenders (i.e., the Troika) of the indebted countries because their governments spending was increasing and their tax revenues have declined, which have led to growing budget deficits. Also, bank nationalizations appeared to have been limited to a few cases, even though that banks are responsible for the global financial crisis. Latvia nationalized its Parex Bank and there are some other

Christian Europe. European leaders are also responsible for the crises that were created in Middle East and North Africa.

[189] We have to do something to right the sinking ship of the economy (as opposed to the conservative plan of letting it fix itself with a few business tax cuts). The first priority are humans (citizens of the country) and then the other secondary objectives (economic philosophies, international obligations, allies, agreements, international institutions, markets, etc.).

[190] See, http://www.politico.com/agenda/story/2015/07/9-myths-about-the-greek-crisis-000131.

[191] See, http://roarmag.org/2014/07/greece-privatization-resistance-movements/.

developing countries. This first global financial crisis of the 21st century will force countries to new reforms and will enhance privatizations (expropriations of the national wealth). Citizens will lose their public and personal wealth and they are not responsible for this planned global crisis. They are the victims of the fool politicians that they fell in the trap of enormous debts with low interest rate, but the lenders know what they are doing, they raise the interest rate to 48.6%, when the debt reached a specific level, as they did for Greece[192]. The Greek Prime Minister, Alexis Tsipras, met with prospective investors in the "Clinton Global Initiative" in New York on September 28, 2015 asking them to go and invest in Greece, which shows that reforms in response to the crisis will improve the climate for privatization[193].

Unfortunately, enforced privatization has become, lately, a nightmare for the indebted Greece and her risk-averse citizens[194]. Assessment of the comparative performance of the different enterprises owned by private firms (POEs) or by governments (SOEs) is basically impossible; first, due to the complexity and social effects and second, due to political pressure and expediency. The Euro-zone had evolved surprisingly quickly (overshooting) into one of the most attractive hotly contested financial markets, through privatization, in the world and it is forcing Euro-zone member-nations and mainly, Greece through the Troika (the Institutions and now, the Quartet) to sell off all their national wealth; but, what will be the social benefits or the social welfare for the nations? By pure economic measures, we might say that in the past, there was economic welfare, but there was no social one. Now, this expropriation of the national wealth is just a huge destruction for Greece and her citizens. The Euro-zone's leftist critics are right: Privatization is a capitalist or more fashionably, "neoliberal" project[195]. Employment has also been negatively affected and it is becoming worse (in Greece 50% was the unemployment among young people and 25.96% the average unemployment rate in March 2015)[196]. The Euro-zone with its austerity measures might had

---

[192] The Greece Government Bond 10Y averaged 7.84% from 1998 until 2015, but, they reached an all-time high of 48.60% in March of 2012 and a record low of 3.21% in June of 2005.

[193] It is a little strange to see leftish government to be forced to sell off the Greek SOEs, now, that the prices are so low. Unfortunately, the third memorandum requires an extra loan of €86 billion; these "neo-liberal" policies have destroyed nations, which was their objective; then, these imposed policies proved to be "very successful." Governments have no power to reject these anti-humane policies (TV News *MEGA*, September 28, 2015).

[194] See, http://eprints.lse.ac.uk/31089/1/GreeSE_No41.pdf.

[195] See, http://www.wsj.com/articles/next-test-for-greeces-tsipras-privatization-1437338474.

[196] See, http://www.tradingeconomics.com/greece/unemployment-rate. The Euro-zone had an official average unemployment rate of 11.00% in August 2015. The true unemployment might be much higher.

created some opportunities for the financial markets and an insignificant revenue for the governments; but, its overvalued common currency, the loss of public policies of the members[197], and the giving up of their sovereignty have caused the cost to exceed the benefits. Thus, we cannot assert that with privatization, we will benefit from the high liquidity, which is created in the financial markets. Greece is forcefully losing her public wealth without receiving any significant amount to pay her debt because the prices are very low (undervalued).

The current excessive privatizations have been motivated by a range of different subjective goals and imposed "objectives"; many have nothing to do with efficiency or social welfare. Some goals are fiscal; raising money from the sale of public enterprises (SOEs) in order to reduce deficits and pay for the current government expenditures, due to its inefficient management and tax evasion by the corrupted businesses. Some other goals are collectible; to gather money and pay off at least the outrageous usurious interest on the outstanding loans. Also, the economic importance of the governments will be reduced and the private firms (multinationals) will take over (economic imperialism, globalization, unemployment, etc.) the entire national wealth. Greeks are led by the Quartet as sheep for slaughter[198].

These unreasonable privatizations are part of the austerity measures that the Troika has imposed and continues to enforce more restrictions and cuts from all the sectors of the economy on the indebted nations, which made the recession worse. They want to test the citizens' reaction, regarding these imposed rules for their "planned" first global financial crisis, which caused the debt crises in EU, and the Greek Parliament passed a law, with which it was hoped the state will raise about $50 billion over the next years from privatization. Lenders have put Greece's public wealth as collateral for their loans[199]. The poor Greek government has to pass these measures to qualify for the next installment of emergency loan from the Quartet [IMF, ECB, European Commission, and the European Stability Mechanism (ESM, the EU's bailout fund)] to finance her current expenses (government spending). In the future these loans with an extremely high interest rate will have to be paid back.

---

[197] "In the eyes of the skeptics, each country is better off setting its own interest rates at levels appropriate for local conditions." See, Wynne and Koech (2012, 1).

[198] See, https://christianvivliografia.wordpress.com/2015/09/16/%cf%89%cf%83-%cf%80%cf%81%ce%bf%ce%b2%ce%b1%cf%84%ce%b1-%ce%b5%cf%80%ce%b9-%cf%83%cf%86%ce%b1%ce%b3%ce%b7%ce%bd-%ce%bc%ce%bf%ce%bd%ce%bf%ce%bd%ce%ba%ce%b1%e1%bd%b6-%ce%bc%ce%bf%ce%bd%ce% bf%ce%bd/.

[199] See, http://www.politico.eu/article/greek-privatization-doomed-to-fail-eurozone-creditors-bail-out/.

There is only one place, from where the government can attain revenue and that is from tax payers (the middle class because wealthy individuals and businesses do not pay taxes). But, the economy is in a deep recession and with all these austerities, there will be no growth, so the disposable income is falling every day. Thus, there is no way for the tax revenue to increase because the personal income is very low, due to reduction in salaries and wages and they put high property taxes and VAT, too. For this reason, along with tax increases, there will also be large scale privatizations (expropriations of the national wealth), if it will be anything left from the previous and current privatizations. Also, now that the stock market is so bad (assets are underpriced), the sales of the SOEs will be at very low prices. Then, privatization must be avoided completely during this period; but, even the new leftish government of SYRIZA was submitted to the new Quartet.

Actually, the SOEs belong to the citizens (tax payers and the loan payers) and not to the governments. Citizens have paid for the construction of their public sector utilities and infrastructure through money acquired by force (high taxes), so the government should have no right to ownership of them. How a government is giving away something, which belongs to the citizens? In reality, creditors are extorting the government to sell off the wealth of the citizens. This is completely unethical and unconstitutional and must be prohibited by the national justice system (Supreme Court). As time goes on, despite the ability of them to forcibly extract money, i.e., from Greece, the revenue from privatization is so small and will decline further, as time goes on; then, the country will go more and more into debt because of her negative growth (deep recession).

Finally, citizens of Europe and especially of historic Greece need "good life self-sufficiency"[200], which includes sufficient work, sufficient property ownership, sufficient wealth, sufficient education, sufficient leisure time, sufficient progress, sufficient independence, and sufficient freedoms. Greeks need to reach human excellence (perfection) and they need self-sufficiency, security, safety, certainty, and sovereignty for developing virtues. Then, citizens need private property ownership and nations need public property ownership. State ownership makes people to be co-owners and cultivate civil friendships, love, patriotism, and become involved in the life of the country (homeland, nation). The end of an Aristotelian democracy is liberty and

[200] Even Aristotle understood self-sufficiency, which build state stability. A person must participate in the activities of the state in order to achieve his natural end and love it, as his own country. The ideal city (state) supports "mere life, it exists for the sake of a good life" (Aristotle, *Politics*, 1252b27-1253a1).

equality. Of course, five centuries later, Greeks adopted new superior virtues, compared to their previous moral, ethical, and philosophical ones, through revelation (their Orthodox faith). We expect people to reach, through work, a certain level of self-sufficiency, but privatization eliminates their right to work and confines their national wealth. Thus, we have to find the optimal level of privatization that maximizes the social welfare. This is the point where the marginal benefits of privatization (revenue to the government, efficiency of the private sector, reduction of deficits and debt, increase in liquidity of the financial market) is equal to the marginal cost of a socio-economic distress (increase in unemployment, loss of income and public wealth, dependency on foreign capital, private monopolists, higher prices, high risk, bail out cost, loss of sovereignty): ($MB_P = MC_{SED}$). European and mainly, Greek politicians have an enormous obligation towards their historic nation and citizens; and for this reason, they have to say "NO" to the forced expropriation of the nation's wealth. They have to send the controlled by the New Agers Quartet back, where it came from, to stop payments on these usurious loans (debts), to leave the Euro-zone, and to find other allies with common values (but not with common currency). By following these recommended policies, there would be no need for any expropriation of the national wealth. Euro-zone and its common currency (euro) is the worst innovation so far, the prototype of the common global currency and global control of all the nations.

REFERENCES

Ackrill, J. L and J. O. Urmson. 1998. Aristotle. *Nicomachean Ethics*. Translated by David Ross. New York City: Oxford University Press.

Alexiou, Constantinos. 2003. "Reflections on Macroeconomic Policy and European Unemployment after Maastricht: Some Evidence." *Spoudai*, 53 (1): 13-36.

Becker, Peter. 2007. Privatizing Public Enterprises in the European Union – The Impact of European Integration on European Water Markets. *SWP Stiftung Wissenschaft und Politik*, Research Unit EU Integration, Berlin: German Institute for International and Security Affairs, December, 1-20.

Bhaskar, V. and Mushtaq Khan. 1995. "Privatization and Employment: A Study of the Jute Industry in Bangladesh." *The American Economic Review*, 85(1): 267-273.

Bullard, James, Christopher J. Neely and David C. Wheelock. 2009. "Systemic Risk and the Financial Crisis: A Primer." *Review*, Federal Reserve Bank of St. Louis, 91(5): 403-417.

Drogalis, Christina. 2008. "Aristotle and the American Social Welfare State." *Trinity*, 1(2): 5-20.

Ignatiou, Michael (Μιχάλης Ἰγνατίου). 2015. *Τρόϊκα: Ὁ Δρόμος πρός τήν Καταστροφή* (Troika: The Road to Destruction) Ἀθήνα: Ἐκδοτικός Οἶκος Α. Α. Λιβάνη (Athens: Livani Publishing. A. Livani).

Kallianiotis, I. N. 2015a. "Economic Policy of Alexander the Great," unpublished manuscript, University of Scranton, September, pages 73.

Kallianiotis, I. N. 2015b. "Fed's Target Rate versus Banks' Deposits and Loans Rates." *Journal of Business Management and Economics* 3(4), April: 7-28. http://innovativejournal.in/jbme/index.php/jbme/article/view/68.

Kallianiotis, I. N. 2015c. <<Ἑλλάς (1832-2015): Τό Βαυαρο-Γερμανικόν Προτεκτορᾶτον>>. (Greece (1832-2015) The Bavaria-German protectorate) Christian Vivliografia, October 21: 1-5. https://christianvivliografia.wordpress.com/2015/10/21/%e1%bc%91%ce%bb%ce%bb%ce%ac%cf%82-1832-2015-%cf%84%cf%8c-%ce%b2%ce%b1%cf%85%ce%b1%cf%81%ce%bf-%ce%b3%ce%b5%cf%81%ce%bc%ce%b1%ce%bd%ce%b9%ce%ba%cf%8c%ce%bd-%cf%80%cf%81%ce%bf%cf%84%ce%b5%ce%ba%cf%84/.

Kallianiotis, I. N. 2015d. "The European Economic Crisis in a Global Context and its Originator," *Archives of Business Research* 3(4), August: 161-171. http://scholarpublishing.org/index.php/ABR/article/view/1407/774.

Kallianiotis, I. N. 2014a. "The Optimal Interest Rates and the Current Interest Rate System." *Eurasian Journal of Economics and Finance* 2(3): 1-25. http://eurasianpublications.com/Eurasian-Journal-of-Economics-and-Finance/Vol.-2-No.3-2014.aspx.

Kallianiotis, I. N. 2014b. *The Greek Contribution to the World*, unpublished manuscript, University of Scranton, December, pages 212.

Kallianiotis, John N. 2013a. *Exchange Rates and International Financial Economics: History, Theories, and practices.* New York: Palgrave MacMillan.

Kallianiotis, John N. 2013b. *International Financial Transactions and Exchange Rates: Trade, Investment, and Parities.* New York, N.Y., US: Palgrave MacMillan.

Kallianiotis, I. N. 2013c. "Privatization in Greece and its Negative Effects on the Nation's Social Welfare (Expropriation of the National Wealth)." *Journal of Business and Economic Studies* 19(1): 1-23.

Kallianiotis, I. N. 2012. "Privatization and Financial Markets in European Union: A Social Welfare Perspective." In: *Social Welfare*, edited by Laratta Rosario, 25-60. Rijeka, Croatia: InTech Publishing.

Kallianiotis, I. N. 2011a. "The Financial and Public Policy of Greece as a Member of the Economic and Monetary Union." Unpublished manuscript, University of Scranton, July, pages 36.

Kallianiotis, I. N. 2011b. "The Latest 'Planned' Financial Crisis, which Caused the First Depression of the 21st Century was a Moral and Political Crisis." Unpublished manuscript, University of Scranton, August, pages 155.

Kallianiotis, I. N. 2011c. "Privatization and its Effects on Financial Markets and their Consequences on Social Welfare." Unpublished manuscript, University of Scranton, November, pages 85.

Kallianiotis, Ioannis N. 2009. "European Privatization and its Effect on Financial Markets and the Economy from a Social Welfare Perspective." *International Research Journal of Finance and Economics* 28: 66-85.

Kallianiotis, Ioannis N. 2007a. "Economic Fundamentals, Expediency, or Naïve Speculation Caused the Euro's Overvaluation." unpublished manuscript, *University of Scranton*, November, pages 44.

Kallianiotis, Ioannis N. 2007b. "Macroeconomic Shocks and Public Policy Effectiveness in Open Economies: US. and European Union." *2007 Conference Proceedings of NBEA*, Central Connecticut State University, New Britain, CT, November 8-9: 164-167.

Kallianiotis, I. N. and Brandon Dragone. 2009. "Privatization and Financial Markets in European Union." In: *Contemporary Issues of Economic and Financial Integration: A Collection of Empirical Work*, edited by Panagiotis Andrikopoulos, 355-370. Athens, Greece: Athens Institute for Education and Research.

Kay, J. and D. Thompson. 1986. "Privatization: A Policy in Search of a Rationale." *Economic Journal*, 96: 18-38.

Kikeri, S., J. Nellis and M. Shirley. 1992. *Privatization: The Lesson of Experience.* Washington, D.C., US: The World Bank.

Luechinger, Simon, Stephan Meier and Alois Stutzer. 2008. "Why Does Unemployment Hurt the Employed? Evidence from the Life Satisfaction Gap between the Private and Public Sectors." *Research Review*, Federal Reserve Bank of Boston 9: 4-6.

Metallinos, George Fr. (Πρωτοπρ. Γεώργιος Δ. Μεταλληνός). (Protopresbyter. George W. Metallinos) 1992. *Λόγος ὡς Ἀντίλογος: Θεολογικά Δοκίμια.* (Speaking as controversy: Theological Essays) Athens: Armos Publishers.

Morgen, Sandra. 2001. "The Agency of Welfare Workers: Negotiating Devolution, Privatization, and the Meaning of Self-sufficiency." *American Anthropologist*, 103(3): 747-762.

Parker, David. 1999. "Privatization in the European Union: A Critical Assessment of its Development, Rationale and Consequences." *Economic and Industrial Democracy* 20(1): 9-38.

Rickards, James. 2014. *The Death of Money: The Coming Collapse of the International Monetary System*, New York, N.Y.: Portfolio/Penguin.

Sack, Brian. 1998. "Does the Fed Act Gradually? A VAR Analysis." Finance and Economics Discussion Series, 1998-17, Board of Governors of the Federal Reserve System.

Sachs, Jeffrey. 2008. "Common Wealth: Economics for a Crowded Planet." Keynote Address at Harvard University, *Alumni Quarterly Colloquy*, Summer: 2-5.

Sappington, D. E. M. and J. E. Stiglitz. 1987. "Privatization, Information and Incentives." *Journal of Policy Analysis and Management* 6: 567-582.

Sposi, Michael and Valerie Grossman. 2014. "Deindustrialization Redeploys Workers to Growing Service Sector." *Economic Letter*, Dallas Fed, 9(11), September: 1-4.

Stiglitz, Joseph E. 2002. *Globalization and its Discontents.* New York: W.W. Norton and Company.

Wessel, David. 2009. *In Fed we Trust.* New York, NY, US: Crown Business.

Williamson, Stephen D. 2014. "Monetary Policy in the United States: A Brave New World?" *Review*, Federal Reserve Bank of St. Louis, 96(2): 111-121.

Wortzel, H. and L. Wortzel. 1989. "Privatization: Not the only Answer." *World Development*: 633-641.

Wynne, Mark A. 2015. "Greece's Fiscal Woes among Issues Hobbling Euro Zone Rebound." *Southwest Economy*, Dallas Fed, Third Quarter: 8-9.

Wynne, Mark A. and Janet Koech. 2012. "One-Size-Fits-All Monetary Policy: Europe and the US" *Economic Letter* 7(9): 1-4.

In: Privatization
Editor: Amelia Hansen

ISBN: 978-1-63484-749-0
© 2016 Nova Science Publishers, Inc.

Chapter 2

EXAMINING EUROPEAN PRIVATISATION PROCESSES AND FIRM PERFORMANCE

Laura Cabeza-García[1,*], Sonia Medina-Salgado[2], María Sacristán-Navarro[2] and Silvia Gómez-Ansón[3]

[1]University of León, Leon, Spain
[2]Rey Juan Carlos University, Madrid, Spain
[3]University of Oviedo, Oviedo, Asturias, Spain

ABSTRACT

This paper analyses different factors that may explain the changes in European firms' performance following privatisation. Using a sample of firms privatised through Share Issue Privatisation (SIP) in six countries in the period 1985-2005, our results demonstrate an improvement in firm efficiency for a long term horizon of five years after privatisation. However, the findings suggest that it is not privatisation *per se* but other factors that matter. We find that the greater the relinquishment of State control, the better the firms' post-privatisation performance, and that privatisations which take place in regulated industries and in non-common law countries seem to show higher levels of efficiency.

Keywords: privatisation, performance, determinants, legal origin

* Facultad de Ciencias Económicas y Empresariales, Campus de Vegazana s/n 24071 León (Spain), Email: laura.cabeza@unileon.es.

Introduction

Over the last few decades, privatisation of State-Owned Enterprises (SOEs) has become a key area of public policy debate and a major economic phenomenon in economies across the world. There has been no sign of a slow-down in the movement towards privatisation. In fact, the global financial crisis has engendered private-sector government involvement in countries previously unfamiliar with this ownership structure (Borisova and Megginson, 2011). Since 2009, global privatisation has exceeded $1.1 trillion, with countries such as China, Australia, Turkey, Greece, Italy and the United Kingdom being very active (Privatization Barometer, 2014). The economic crisis has seen privatisation placed high on the agenda of the "troika" of supranational bodies' (the EU, the European Central Bank and the IMF) programmes, and in the context of budget consolidation and reforms. In Europe, privatisation of SOEs has been one of the tools employed, or at least considered, by governments to improve the public deficit and other economic indicators. For instance, the largest Share Issue Privatisation (SIP) in 2013 was that of the Greek bank Piraeus, a privatisation on which the troika insisted. More recently, one of the key terms of Greece's 86 billion euro reform-for-aid package agreed was its privatisation trust fund, into which Athens will transfer around 50 billion euros worth of State assets. One of the ways to monetise these assets will be to privatise them. This recent and current trend towards privatisation has kept alive the policy debate around privatisation, and supports the need to better understand the underlying reasons that may explain the success of privatisation.

The goals underlying privatisation processes are diverse, including financial, political and economic objectives (Cuervo, 1997). Financial reasons relate to revenues obtained by States when selling formerly SOEs (Vickers and Yarrow, 1988) and the benefits that accrue from eliminating subsidies to SOEs. Political reasons for privatising SOEs rest on the purported weaknesses inherent in State ownership. Economic motivations for privatisation are based on claims that private companies outperform their State-owned counterparts. Whether financial, political or economic reasons are put forward to justify privatisations, pro-privatisation arguments are supported by the results of different studies suggesting that private ownership leads to higher levels of productivity and to superior efficiency and performance than State ownership (Cuervo and Maroto, 1983; Ehrlich et al., 1994; Argimon et al., 1999; Dewenter and Malatesta, 2001; Ng and Seabright, 2001), and that privatisations have led to significant increases in productivity and profitability

(Megginson et al., 1994; Boubakri and Cosset, 1998; D' Souza et al., 2007). However, other studies suggest that privatisations do not seem to lead to systematic improvements in firms' efficiency or performance (for instance, Vickers and Yarrow, 1988; Bishop and Thomson, 1992; Pestieau and Tulkens, 1993; González-Páramo, 1995; Martin and Parker, 1995; Dewenter and Malatesta, 2001; Reeves and Palcic, 2004)[1]. As Megginson and Netter (2001) point out, the different results may be due to methodology, samples, or differences in measurement.

Privatised firms' performance and contribution to growth may also vary according to societal and institutional arrangements (Marcelin and Mathur, 2015). The majority of existing empirical studies regarding privatisations have focused on one single country (Yarrow, 1989 and Martin and Parker, 1995 – United Kingdom; Boardman et al., 2002 – Canada), or have used sample firms privatised in both developed and developing countries (Megginson et al., 1994; D'Souza et al., 2005), just in developing countries (Boubakri and Cosset, 1998; Boubakri et al., 2005a), just in developed countries (D'Souza and Megginson, 1999), or in Eastern European countries (Claessens and Djankov, 2002; Brown et al., 2006). However, as far as we know, few studies have analysed privatisation performance improvements in a European context. An exception is Arcas and Bachiller (2010), although these authors do not specifically include institutional environment as a determinant of divested firms' performance[2].

Divested firms' control rights, deregulations, and increases in competition should also be considered when analysing privatisation processes (Li and Xu, 2004; Boubakri et al., 2005b; D'Souza et al., 2005). These factors may also be linked to a country's institutional setting. As Boubakri et al., (2011) report, the political system and political issues, for instance, are important determinants of State ownership in privatised firms. Consequently, as Marcelin and Mathur (2015) point out, it is important to analyse the links between divested firms' performance along the dimensions of property rights protection and institutional quality.

Our paper aims to respond to this need for further research into how the characteristics of the country and firm in question influence the performance

[1] For a survey of the privatisation literature, see Megginson and Netter (2001), Djankov and Murell (2002) or Estrin et al. (2009). In addition, Denisova et al. (2012) analyse public opinion regarding privatisation.

[2] In comparison with Arcas and Bachiller (2010), our period of study is larger and includes more recent privatisations. In addition, we employ a larger number of proxies of firm performance and include more determinants of divested firms' performance, in particular, the institutional environment.

of privatised firms. To do this, we analyse the effects of privatisation on companies' performance and possible determinants of performance changes in privatised firms in Europe over the course of a large time period, looking at firms involved in the wave of privatisations that began in the 1980s and ended before the subprime crisis. The sample comprises SOEs privatised in six European countries: Finland, France, Germany, Spain, Sweden and the United Kingdom. The six chosen countries belong to the four different legal origins present in Europe: Scandinavian (Finland and Sweden), French Civil Law (France and Spain), German Civil Law (Germany) and Common Law (United Kingdom), and therefore represent all European legal traditions. The diversity of the chosen countries' legal origins allows us to test the influence of institutional environment as a determinant of divested firms' performance. We also consider how State control rights – an aspect closely linked to political institutions, political systems and constraints (Boubakri et al., 2011, 2015) – and competition affect firms' performance. Using a sample of SIPs between 1985 and 2005 in these six countries, and employing a panel data methodology, which allows us to control for firm-specific heterogeneity (most of the empirical studies employ ordinary least squares analyses[3]), we analyse changes in firm performance after privatisation and whether State control rights after privatisation, competition and institutional environment influence the observed changes.

Contrary to the current thinking and previous empirical evidence reported by different authors for multi-country samples, our results show no evidence of significant post-privatisation improvements in firms' profitability (either for the multi-country European sample or for the individual countries' sub-samples). Neither, when considering each country individually, do they find evidence of significant improvement in divested firms' efficiency, although results for the multi-country sample do suggest significant improvements in divested firms' efficiency after privatisation. Our results thus suggest that it is not privatisation *per se* that drives firm performance. In line with the survey by Estrin et al., (2009) and Cabeza-García and Gómez-Ansón (2012), our results support the claim that the State's relinquishment of control in firms' capital enhances post-privatisation profitability and efficiency, and that in divested firms belonging to regulated industries and to non-common law countries firm

[3] Some exceptions that employ panel data methodology are Villalonga (2000) and Cabeza-García and Gómez-Ansón (2012) for Spain, Alexandre and Charreaux (2004) for France, Bortolotti et al. (2002) and Li and Xu (2004) for international samples in the telecommunications sector, and Brown et al. (2006), Ausseneg and Jelic (2007) and Brown et al. (2010) for Eastern European countries.

profitability and efficiency increases are higher. These results support the idea that the benefits of privatisation are driven by private ownership and management, in opposition to the inefficiency traditionally attributed to public ownership and management (Arocena and Oliveros, 2012), due to increases in competition and higher monitoring by the market, especially in non-common law countries.

The remainder of the paper is organised as follows. Section 2 describes the consequences of privatisation processes on firm performance, and surveys the theoretical and empirical literature regarding potential sources of improved operating performance post-privatisation. Section 3 describes the sample selection, methodology and variables employed. The results are discussed in Section 4, and Section 5 presents the main conclusions of the paper.

THEORETICAL ARGUMENTS AND HYPOTHESES

Privatisation theory predicts higher levels of performance from private firms and privatisations (Yarrow, 1986; Boycko et al., 1993) due to the inefficiency of governments as shareholders and managers, and the non-profit and value-maximising objectives that SOEs may pursue (Megginson and Netter, 2001). Public firms are expected to be more risk-averse and less free in their decision-making (Frydman et al., 2000), and agency-related problems may be more severe (SOEs face a dual level of agency relations – citizens-government and government-management – and are not subject to market and bankruptcy discipline). In addition, SOEs may pursue political goals aimed at maximising social welfare which may be inconsistent with efficiency, and market pressures and reduction of State subsidies should drive privatised firms to employ their human, financial and technological resources more efficiently (Boycko et al., 1993).

Accordingly, different empirical studies report an increase in the ratios of return on assets and return over sales for privatised firms (Megginson et al., 1994; Boubakri and Cosset, 1998; Antoncic and Hisrich, 2003; D'Souza et al., 2007) and in a firm's efficiency (De Alessi, 1980; Vining and Boardman, 1992; D' Souza and Megginson, 1999; Sun and Tong, 2003; D'Souza et al., 2005 and 2007; Arocena and Oliveros, 2012[4]).

[4] For a sample of SOEs privatised in Spain, Arocena and Oliveros (2012) find that the efficiency of newly privatised firms significantly increased after their privatisation while private competitors showed no significant improvement during the same post-privatisation period.

Considering these arguments, we propose the following hypothesis:

H1: A firm's profitability and operating efficiency increase after privatisation.

However, in addition to the privatisation *per se*, other factors may also influence divested firms' performance. For instance, State control rights and the competitive and institutional environments. Regarding State control rights, governments are thought to distort managerial objectives for political gain, and therefore when control rights[5] pass from the State to private investors the firm's objectives and managerial incentives are redefined and performance improves (Boycko et al., 1996). Accordingly, privatised firms where the State maintains majority ownership are more likely to delay restructuring and to be more averse to layoffs (Claessens et al., 1997). Moreover, managers of divested companies controlled by the State may not have incentives to take risks, and might pursue non-value-maximising objectives (Shleifer and Vishny, 1996). In addition, SOEs have difficulty overseeing their managers because there is neither an individual owner with strong incentives to do so nor a public price for providing information about good or bad managers (Laffont and Tirole, 1993). In line with these arguments, the empirical evidence tends to support the existence of an inverse relationship between State ownership and firm performance both for developing countries (D'Souza and Megginson, 1999), for China (Wei et al., 2003) and developed countries (D'Souza et al., 2007). Moreover, for a sample of 47 countries Faccio (2010) shows that companies with political connections, especially though ownership, have more leverage and higher market shares, but that they underperform in comparison with non-connected companies.

Considering these arguments and prior empirical evidence, we expect:

H2: The lower the State stakes in firms' capital, the better the privatised company's profitability and efficiency will be.

Competitive environments may also be crucial to the success of privatisations (Harper, 2002) as they may be more conducive to the monitoring of managers, offering them incentives to maximise shareholder wealth (Shirley and Nellis, 1991; Grosse and Yanes, 1998). Consequently, price deregulations

[5] The State may retain control by ownership, but also by using politically connected firms or golden shares.

and market liberalisations that put pressure on managers to maximise shareholder wealth and reduce political interference should lead to improvements in the performance of privatised companies. Previous studies confirm this: Sheshinski and López-Calva (2003) report that the more concentrated and/or regulated a market, the smaller the increase in a firm's productivity, and Megginson et al., (1994) and La Porta and López de Silanes (1999) show that the improvements in efficiency seem to be larger for privatised firms that operate in competitive markets. Therefore, we propose hypothesis 3:

H3: The greater the firm's market competitiveness, the better the privatised company's profitability and efficiency.

The third factor which may influence the success of privatisation that we consider is the institutional environment, and specifically the legal origin of the country of the privatised firm. Following La Porta et al., (1997; 1998), shareholders and creditors' rights vary depending on the legal tradition, with common law countries showing greater protection of shareholders' rights. Shareholders' rights also determine capital market development. In particular, better investor protection is associated with improved financial development, better access to finance and lighter government ownership and regulation (La Porta et al., 2008). Additionally, Pagano and Roell (1998) argue that greater legal protection of investor rights hinders collusion between the firm and potential monitors and promotes more effective managerial monitoring, and that, consequently, better performance should be expected. Thus, privatisations in common law countries, countries with greater protection of shareholders' rights, should lead to higher levels of improvement in divested firms' performance. However, the empirical evidence, although scarce, does not tend to support this prediction. D'Souza et al., (2007) report that the higher the level of shareholders protection the lower the increase in privatised firms' sales and employment, and that profitability and efficiency do not seem to be related to shareholders' rights; similarly, D'Souza et al., (2005) do not find that legal origin has a significant effect on firm profitability and efficiency.

In addition, when analysing the influence of legal tradition on privatised firm performance, one should also consider how legal tradition may influence the government incentives to relinquish control of SOEs (La Porta et al., 1997; 1998), especially given that in civil law countries the State is a more influential block holder (La Porta et al., 1999)[6], and that weaker protection of shareholders would lead to lower market values at privatisation discouraging full privatisations. For instance, Bortolotti and Faccio (2009) report that, in civil law countries, States are more likely to retain control through ownership and to be the largest blockholder in privatised firms, while in common law countries, States more frequently tend to use golden shares in order to retain control.

Considering these arguments, and the fact that common law countries tend to provide a stronger protection of shareholder rights and to retain less State ownership in privatised firms, we predict that firms privatised in common law countries should exhibit stronger performance improvements:

H4: Divested firms that belong to common law countries will show higher profitability and efficiency.

SAMPLE, METHODOLOGY AND VARIABLES

Sample Selection

The initial database used for our analysis comprised 116 non-financial and non-insurance companies privatised through SIPs in six European countries (Finland, France, Germany, Spain, Sweden and the United Kingdom) in the period between 1980 and 2005. While governments may use other methods of privatisation (e.g., direct sales), SIPs represent the largest and most economically and politically important privatisations. The information needed to construct the initial database was obtained from the Privatization Barometer database.

We attempted to obtain financial information about the divested firms for a period of up to 11 years, encompassing five years prior to the first stage or block of privatisation and five years after the last stage or block of privatisation. The information was obtained from Datastream and Osiris databases, the companies' websites, and directly from the companies. In addition, exchange rates were obtained from the information provided by the

[6] In this sense, La Porta et al. (2008) also show that civil law countries are generally associated with lower shareholder and creditor protection and higher government ownership of banks and higher State ownership of the media.

Spanish Central Bank (*Banco de España*). Excluding companies for which we could not obtain information, the sample amounts to 95 SIPs (Table 1)[7].

Table 1. Sample description

Country	Firms	Privatisation processes	State stake (1S)	State stake (LS)	% Regulated firms
Finland	10	16	56.040%	48.158%	40% (4 firms)
France	22	29	41.906%	37.095%	41% (9 firms)
Germany	10	13	47.604%	43.751%	70% (7 firms)
Spain	15	19	48.206%	40.695%	60% (9 firms)
Sweden	7	9	34.585%	32.398%	14.28% (1 firm)
UK	31	35	46.242%	43.278%	84% (26 firms)
Total	95	121	45.906%	41.244%	59% (56 firms)

1S and LS denote first and last stage of privatisation.
Source: Own elaboration.

SOEs may be sold in stages, and the first and last stages may be of particular interest. The first stage initiates the privatisation trend, signalling the State's commitment to divesting the firm, and the change from public to private ownership may be more active at this stage. In the final stage, State relinquishment of control is at its highest, and therefore higher improved firm profitability and efficiency should be expected. Thus, we considered both the first and last stage of privatisations, ending up with 121 privatisation processes. 59% of the processes refer to utilities[8], and as a mean the State retains more than a 40% of firms' capital.

[7] However, it is worth noting that although the sample amounts to 95 SIPs, due to the necessity of having no missing values in dependent and explanatory variables for at least four consecutive years (complete but unbalanced panel), the final sample's size in the models varies between 75 and 78 firms, while the total number of observations varies between 651 and 652. The observations are not the same in both stages of privatisation as for some firms, especially those privatised in stages, it was not possible to obtain information for both stages of privatisation. Nevertheless, the samples used in the regressions models maintain the proportion of firms privatised in the majority of the countries, with the proportion for the United Kingdom and France slightly lower (approximately 50% of the privatised firms).

[8] In this sense, there is no bias in our sample: 60.34% of the firms belong to a regulated industry. Nevertheless, it is necessary to point out that, both in the whole database and in our sample, the distribution among the different countries it is not the same: the United Kingdom is the country with more privatised firms in regulated industries (84% of the cases in our sample and in the whole database), followed by Germany (70% of the cases), Spain (60% of the cases), France (41% in the sample and 40% in the database), Finland (40% in the sample and 45% in the database) and Sweden (14%).

Methodology and Variables

In line with the first hypothesis proposed in the previous section, the first objective of our paper is to study whether the privatisation of SOEs leads to an increase in firms' profitability and efficiency. We follow Megginson et al., (1994), Boubakri and Cosset (1998), and D'Souza and Megginson (1999) in using a matched pairs methodology (pre- versus post-privatisation). Empirical proxies for each variable and each company are computed for a period of up to 11 years, including the five years before and five years after the last stage of privatisation. Thus, the different performance proxies from the five years of public ownership through to the end of the first five years as a privatised entity (both for the first stage of the privatisation – 1S – and the last stage of the privatisation – LS) are estimated for each company. The mean and median of each variable for each firm over the pre- and post-privatisation windows are then calculated. For all firms, the year of privatisation is named year 0. As this includes both public and private ownership phases of the enterprise, it is excluded from the calculations. Having computed pre- and post- privatisation mean and median values, we use the Student's t-test and the Wilcoxon Signed Rank test to test for significant changes in the variables.

Table 2 (Panel A) shows the performance variables used in the study. We measure profitability using three ratios: return on assets (ROA), return on equity (ROE) and return on sales (ROS). We test for changes in operating efficiency by analysing four ratios: sales-to-employees (SALES/EMP), net profit-to-employees (NP/EMP), operating profit-to-employees (OP/EMP) and added value-to-employees (AV/EMP).

Next, we relate the different proxies for a company's profitability and operating efficiency to the set of proxy variables that relate to hypotheses 2 to 4 (Table 2, Panel B): *(a)* proxy variable for the State's stakes (STATEOWN), *(b)* a proxy variable for the level of the firms' industry competitiveness (REGINDUSTRY) and *(c)* a proxy variable for the institutional environment (LAWORIGIN)[9]. As control variables we include a proxy variable for the firms' size (LSIZE)[10] and a dummy variable, POSTPRIVAT, which takes on

[9] We are aware of the existence of other more complete and precise measures for the institutional environment, but due to the number of countries included in the study, we decided to consider just this variable.

[10] Larger firms may be more difficult to turn out after privatisation and may benefit from greater ongoing State support; for instance, they may receive soft financing. As a result, larger SOEs may be operating under better economic and financial conditions at the moment of privatisation and, consequently, may exhibit less substantial post-privatisation performance improvements. It can also be argued, however, that their better historical performance,

the value 1 from the privatisation year onward. Thus, we estimate the following regression model[11]:

$$PERFORMANCE_{it} = a_0 + \beta_1 STATEOWN_{it} + \beta_2 REGINDUSTRY_{it} + \beta_3 LAWORIGIN_{it} + \beta_4 LSIZE_{it} + \beta_5 POSTPRIVAT_{it} + \mu_{it}$$

where PERFORMANCE denotes the different proxies for firms' profitability and efficiency, STATEOWN is defined as the size of the State's stake in the firm's capital each year, REGINDUSTRY is a dummy variable that takes on the value of 1 when the firms belong to regulated industries and 0 otherwise[12], LAWORIGIN is a dummy variable that adopts the value of 1 when the firm belongs to a common law country and 0 otherwise, firm size is defined as the logarithm of the firm's total assets each year (LSIZE)[13], and POSTPRIVAT is a dummy variable that takes on the value 1 in the post-privatisation period and 0 otherwise.

These models are estimated via a pooled cross-sectional time-series regression using a generalised least squares (GLS) procedure. Panel data estimations seem to be the most suitable method of capturing performance indicator variations over time, since we can control for individual, firm-specific unobservable heterogeneity as well as temporal changes in a firm's operating environment, and we avoid problems caused by the possible correlation between non-observable firm characteristics and individual variables (Hausman and Taylor, 1981). As is customary in panel data analyses, we estimate both fixed-effects and random-effects models. If the Hausman test is significant, we focus on the fixed-effects model, whereas we stress the random-effects model if the test turns out to be non-significant (Hausman, 1978). Additionally, we correct the estimations for heteroskedasticity problems.

linked to the positive effect of privatisation, could result in better post-privatisation performance in comparison with smaller firms.

[11] The estimations were also made with year dummies, and the results did not vary significantly. However, considering that they increase the number of variables in the models, we prefer to show the results without them.

[12] We repeated the estimations considering industry dummies and the results did not vary significantly. Some of these variables turned out to be significant.

[13] Alternatively, we considered the logarithm of the firm's sales as a proxy variable for the firm's size. The results were similar.

Table 2. Variables of the study

Variables	Description	Predicted relation
Panel A: Dependent variables		
Profitability		
Return on assets (ROA)	Operating profits/total assets	$ROA_A > ROA_B$
Return on equity (ROE)	Net profit/total equity	$ROE_A > ROE_B$
Return on sales (ROS)	Operating profits/sales	$ROS_A > ROS_B$
Operating efficiency		
SALES/EMP	Sales/number of employees	$SALES/EMP_A > SALES/EMP_B$
NP/EMP	Net profit/number of employees	$NP/EMP_A > NP/EMP_B$
OP/EMP	Operating profits/number of employees	$OP/EMP_A > OP/EMP_B$
AV/EMP	Added value/number of employees	$AV/EMP_A > AV/EMP_B$

Panel B: Explanatory and control variables		
Explanatory variables		
STATEOWN	Percentage the State holds in the firm's capital each year	-
REGINDUSTRY	Dummy variable that takes on value 1 if the firm belongs to a regulated industry and 0 otherwise (each year)	-
LAWORIGIN	Dummy variable that takes on value 1 if the firm belongs to a common law country and 0 otherwise (each year)	+
Control variables		
(L)SIZE	(Logarithm) Firm's total assets each year	
POSTPRIVAT	Dummy variable that takes on value 1 within the post-privatisation period and 0 otherwise	

A and B denote after and before privatisation.

SUMMARY STATISTICS AND VARIABLE CORRELATIONS

Summary statistics of key dependent and explanatory variables for the first stage of the privatisation processes are shown in Table 3[14]. Regarding bivariate correlations between variables, variable LSIZE is significantly and positively correlated with variables STATEOWN and REGINDUSTRY, suggesting that the larger the firm the larger the State's stake in privatised firms and that larger firms belong more frequently to regulated industries.

[14] Summary statistics and correlations are shown for the sample used in the regression models. For the last stage of privatisation the summary statistics and bivariate correlations were similar.

Table 3. Summary Statistics (first stage of privatisation)

Variables	Mean	Median	Maximum	Minimum	Stand. Dev.
Dependent variables					
ROA	8.457	7.609	150.350	-30.617	9.945
ROE	8.331	7.889	99.446	-86.456	13.584
ROS	13.067	9.392	84.410	-37.569	13.941
SALES/EMP	0.324	0.210	6.608	0.006	0.544
NP/EMP	0.028	0.009	1.501	-0.485	0.104
OP/EMP	0.048	0.018	3.208	-0.602	0.169
AV/EMP	0.123	0.063	4.955	-0.014	0.295
Explanatory and control variables					
STATEOWN	37.674	33.390	100	0	33.584
SIZE	18,115.08	71.599	301,296.3	12.272	42,400.79
Other explanatory and control variables		Percentage/(number) or observations			
REGINDUSTRY		55.21% (360)			
LAWORIGIN		20.55% (134)			
POSTPRIVAT		53.53% (349)			

The sample consists of 75 European privatised firms during the period 1980-2005 (652 observations).

As expected, the variable POSTPRIVAT is negatively correlated to the variable STATEOWN. LAWORIGIN is negatively and significantly correlated with the State's stake in firms' capital (STATEOWN) but positively with REGINDUSTRY. In common law countries, as suggested by hypothesis 3 and reported by Bortolotti and Faccio (2009), governments are more likely to relinquish control of privatised firms. In addition, privatised firms in common law countries are more likely to belong to a regulated industry (this correlation is due to the large number of privatisations of regulated firms in the United Kingdom. See footnote 8).

Finally, non-common law countries' privatised firms seem to be larger, as suggested by the negative correlation between the LAWORIGIN and LSIZE variables[15].

[15] In all the sample-countries there is a negative correlation between the State's stake and variable POSTPRIVAT. However, there are some differences in the sub-samples in some of the correlations. For instance, the correlation between REGINDUSTRY and LSIZE holds for all of the countries except Germany, and the correlation of STATEOWN and LSIZE does not appear for the United Kingdom, Germany and Spain. There is also a negative correlation between the State stakes in firm capital and firms that belong to regulated industries for Finland, France, Germany and Spain and a positive correlation for Sweden – but no correlation for the sample and the sub-sample of the United Kingdom.

Table 4. Correlation matrix for the dependent and explanatory variables

Variables	1	2	3	4	5	6	7	8	9	10	11
1. ROA	1										
2. ROE	0.529*** (0.000)	1									
3. ROS	0.568*** (0.000)	0.266*** (0.000)	1								
4. SALES/ EMP	0.032 (0.413)	0.082** (0.036)	0.087** (0.026)	1							
5. NP/ EMP	0.101*** (0.000)	0.229*** (0.000)	0.302*** (0.000)	0.777*** (0.000)	1						
6. OP/ EMP	0.178*** (0.000)	0.156*** (0.000)	0.343*** (0.000)	0.711*** (0.000)	0.938*** (0.000)	1					
7. AV /EMP	0.067* (0.083)	0.137*** (0.000)	0.224*** (0.000)	0.901*** (0.000)	0.855*** (0.000)	0.878*** (0.000)	1				
8. STATE-OWN	-0.193*** (0.000)	-0.061 (0.1169	-0.061 (0.116)	-0.102 (0.009)	-0.128*** (0.000)	-0.097** (0.012)	-0.114*** (0.003)	1			
9. REG-INDUSTRY	-0.105*** (0.006)	0.033 (0.388)	0.247*** (0.000)	0.173*** (0.000)	0.186*** (0.000)	0.172*** (0.000)	0.175*** (0.000)	0.049 (0.206)	1		
10. LAW-ORIGIN	0.030 (0.441)	0.082 (0.034)	0.113*** (0.003)	-0.012 (0.748)	0.095** (0.014)	0.055 (0.154)	0.067* (0.086)	-0.295*** (0.000)	0.244*** (0.000)	1	
11. LSIZE	-0.187*** (0.000)	-0.151*** (0.000)	-0.076* (0.051)	0.239*** (0.000)	0.072* (0.074)	0.081** (0.036)	0.110*** (0.004)	0.108*** (0.005)	0.316*** (0.000)	-0.240*** (0.000)	1
12. POST-PRIVAT	0.048 (0.216)	-0.004 (0.913)	0.065* (0.094)	0.010 (0.798)	0.057 (0.141)	0.026 (0.500)	0.009 (0.811)	-0.456*** (0.000)	0.039 (0.320)	0.177*** (0.000)	0.034 (0.375)

The sample consists of 75 European privatised firms during the period 1980-2005.

(P-value) * Statistically significant at the 10% level ** Statistically significant at the 5% level *** Statistically significant at the 1% level.

We must note that although some variables show a statistically significant correlation, when applying variance inflation factors (VIFs) we find no evidence of multicollinearity problems.

RESULTS

European Privatisations and Firms' Profitability and Efficiency

Table 5 shows the mean and median differences in firms' performance after their privatisation over the [-5, +5] years window[16]. We find a significant increase in the mean and median values for all the proxies of efficiency in both stages of privatisation. By contrast, no significant differences are found in firm profitability (ROA, ROE or ROS)[17]. Thus, there seems to be support for hypothesis 1, as the change from public to private ownership, over a long time horizon, leads to increases in firms' efficiency *per se*[18]. In this respect, our results are similar to those reported by Boubakri and Cosset (1998) for a sample of firms privatised in developing countries, by Megginson et al., (1994) and D'Souza and Megginson (1999) for a sample of firms privatised in industrialised countries, by D'Souza et al., (2007) for a sample of 161 companies from 39 countries, and by La Porta and Lopez de Silanes (1999) for Mexico.

However, when wc compare the performance change after privatisation for the sub-sample of privatisations in each country, the results differ. As was the case for the whole sample, we again find no evidence of significant increases in firm profitability after privatisation, but for operating efficiency, not all countries show efficiency improvements. In Spain there is a significant increase in the ratios of sales to employees and net profit to employees in both

---

[16] We focus on the non-parametric Wilcoxon test, since, after applying the Kolmogorov Smirnoff test, the hypothesis of normality of the performance variables is not accepted.

[17] Although it is not shown, we also find a significant increase in the mean and median values in the first stage of privatisation for the firm employment (at 10% level) and a significant decrease for the ratio of long term leverage (LLEV). Regarding firm sales, this decrease after privatisation in the first stage of privatisations, but the opposite occurs for the last stage of privatisations. Thus, there is an increase in firms' sales but a decrease in firms' leverage after privatisation. By contrast, no significant differences were found in firm total leverage.

[18] Over the window [-3, +3] the results were similar: there is a significant increase in all of the proxies of efficiency, sales and employment in both stages of privatisation, and a significant decrease in long term leverage and in total leverage for the last stage.

stages of privatisations and of operating profit to employees in the last stage. Sweden, Finland and France show, at different stages of the privatisation process, an increase in the ratio of sales to employees, and Finland and France also show an improvement in the ratio of added value to employees (during both stages of privatisations). United Kingdom firms only show an increase in the last stage in the ratio of net profit to employees. However, in Germany there is no significant increase in divested firms' efficiency. Thus, non-common law countries (with the exception of Germany) seem to present more significant increases in firm efficiency than the United Kingdom. However, we must be cautious with these results due to the small size of the sub-samples for some countries.

The Influence of State Control, Industry and Legal Environment on European Privatised Firms' Profitability and Efficiency

We next refer to the results of the regression models which analyse how different factors may influence the success of privatisations (see Table 6)[19].

Profitability

The analyses reveal a negative and significant coefficient for the variable STATEOWN on profitability for the first and last stage of privatisations. In addition, the variable REGINDUSTRY presents a positive and significant coefficient for ROE (first stage) and ROS (both stages of privatisations). The type of legislation of the country (LAWORIGIN) does not significantly influence firm profitability. Furthermore, and with regard to the profitability

[19] We also ran all the models including just the proxy variable related to each of the proposed hypotheses. The results were similar: STATEOWN seems to influence firm profitability and efficiency negatively and significantly, REGINDUSTRY does not seem to influence significantly firm profitability but positively and significantly influences firm efficiency. LAWORIGIN does not follow the same trend in all the models, being sometimes positive and other times negative, but in all cases it is not statistically significant. Finally, POSTPRIVAT turned out to be positive in all the models but never presents a significant coefficient. Considering that variable POSTPRIVAT is significantly correlated with variables STATEOWN and LAWORIGIN, these results suggest that it is not privatisation *per se*, but other factors that may drive post-privatisation operating performance improvements. We also carried out comparisons between sub-samples, and the findings show that there is a clearer improvement in firm profitability and efficiency when the State retains less than 50% of the capital, and an improvement in efficiency in regulated industries and in countries with non-common law origin.

ratios (ROA and ROS), the privatisation *per se* (POSTPRIVAT) presents a negative and statistically significant coefficient for ROE and ROA. Finally, the coefficient of firm size (LSIZE) is negative and significant for the profitability ratios ROA and ROS for the first stage of privatisation but positive for the last stage (ROS).

Efficiency

For the last stage of privatisations, the results show that the greater the State's stake in the capital (STATEOWN), the lower the level of firm efficiency (ratio SALES/EMP). For both stages of privatisations, the type of sector (regulated or not) (REGINDUSTRY) has resulted in increased efficiency (ratios SALES/EMP, NP/EMP, OP/EMP and AV/EMP). Another factor worth mentioning is legal origin (LAWORIGIN). Contrary to what was proposed in hypothesis 4, when significant, the coefficient of this variable suggests that firm efficiency increases when the company belongs to a non-common law country. Finally, privatisation *per se* does not seem to have a clear effect on efficiency: the variable POSTPRIVAT does not turn out to be significant. Similarly, firm size does not seem to explain divested firms' efficiency.

SUMMARY OF RESULTS

To sum up, the results do not suggest an increase in divested firms' profitability. Regarding firms' efficiency, although results may suggest that privatisations lead to improvements in divested firms' efficiency, these results do not hold when analysing individually each of the countries included in the study. Furthermore, once other factors that may influence privatised firms' performance are controlled, privatisation *per se* does not significantly influence firm efficiency. Thus, our results do not support hypothesis 1.

The results do support hypothesis 2, that the relinquishment of control by the State enhances firm profitability and efficiency. These findings are similar to those reported by D'Souza and Megginson (1999), Wei et al., (2003), Boubakri et al., (2005b) and D'Souza et al., (2007). Moreover, contrary to what was expected (hypothesis 3), the results suggest that firms belonging to regulated industries demonstrate higher operating efficiency after privatisation. This result contradicts those of previous studies which find no significant influence of industry regulation on privatised firm performance (Harper 2002 for the Czech Republic; D'Souza et al., 2005 for a multi-country sample; Boubakri et al., 2005 for OECD countries) or which report a negative influence of EU industry regulation on firm performance (Arcas and Bachiller, 2010), but is in line with the results reported by D'Souza and Megginson (1999) for a sample of firms privatised in industrialised countries. Similarly, Sun and Tong (2003) for China show a positive and significant effect of regulation on divested firms' real net profit and efficiency. As D'Souza and Megginson (1999) point out, the environment in which electricity and telecommunications firms were operating changed dramatically during the 1990s, and companies in these regulated sectors experienced substantial performance improvements. Thus, it is not possible to determine whether the improvements in performance are the result of privatisation, or whether privatisation performance was driven by the performance enhancements resulting from more profound technological developments and a worldwide swing towards deregulation.

Finally, as was suggested in the comparison between sub-samples, the results also suggest that firms from common law countries experience lower increases in firm efficiency. This finding contradicts the results of D'Souza et al., (2005; 2007), who report, respectively, that the stronger protection of shareholder rights in common law countries may result in more pronounced performance improvements, and that shareholders' rights do not influence privatised firms' profitability and efficiency.

We must note that our results are not a consequence of the observed correlations between legal origin and State ownership and industry regulation, as these variables have already been considered in the regressions. Thus, these results point to the possible existence of omitted variables which may be driving the relation between the legal origin variable and firm profitability and efficiency. Furthermore, we must also take into consideration that the legal origin variable may be a proxy for other factors (culture, history and politics). For instance, the political perspective proposes that legal rules are the product of legislative policy decisions, voters' preferences and interest groups' power.

Table 5. Mean and median differences [-5, +5]

Variable	Pre- privatisation		Post- privatisation		Difference		Z	
	Mean	Median	Mean	Median	Means	Medians	Student's t	Wilcoxon
Profitability								
ROA (1S) n = 47	8.752	6.945	9.304	7.489	0.552	0.544	0.326	-0.265
ROA (LT) n = 47	8.752	6.945	9.342	7.489	0.552	0.544	0.355	-0.138
ROE (1S) n = 48	6.117	5.018	6.983	6.870	0.866	1.852	0.627	-1.067
ROE (LT) n = 48	6.117	5.018	7.704	7.140	1.587	2.122	1.376	-1.221
ROS (1S) n = 48	14.227	9.459	13.640	8.873	-0.587	-0.586	-0.271	-0.123
ROS (LS) n = 48	14.227	9.459	13.586	8.853	-0.641	-0.606	-0.307	-0.277
Efficiency								
SALES/EMP (1S) n = 48	0.223	0.173	0.267	0.228	0.044	0.055	1.872*	-3.282***
SALES/EMP (LT) n = 48	0.223	0.173	0.293	0.228	0.070	0.055	2.654**	-3.836***
NP/EMP (1S) n = 48	0.010	0.005	0.018	0.008	0.008	0.003	2.548**	-2.851***
NP/EMP (LT) n = 48	0.010	0.005	0.020	0.011	0.010	0.006	3.383***	-3.846***
OP/EMP (1S) n = 46	0.026	0.015	0.039	0.020	0.013	0.005	1.865*	-2.070**
OP/EMP (LT) n = 46	0.026	0.015	0.040	0.024	0.014	0.009	2.529**	-3.097***
AV/EMP (1S) n = 35	0.075	0.052	0.086	0.063	0.011	0.011	1.091	-2.146**
AV/EMP (LT) n = 35	0.075	0.052	0.088	0.072	0.013	0.020	1.333	-2.457**

* Statistically significant at the 10% level ** Statistically significant at the 5% level *** Statistically significant at the 1% level.
1S and LS denote first and last stage of privatisation respectively.

Table 6. Performance Determinants of Privatised Firm

Panel A: First stage of privatisations							
Variable	Reg. 1 (ROA)	Reg. 2 (ROE)	Reg. 3 (ROS)	Reg. 4 (SALES/EMP)	Reg. 5 (NP/EMP)	Reg. 6 (OP/EMP)	Reg. 7 (AV/EMP)
Constant	26.164*** (0.000)	31.176* (0.053)	-18.392* (0.088)	0.234 (0.473)	-0.010 (0.255)	0.099 (0.420)	0.238 (0.297)
STATEOWN	-0.040*** (0.001)	-0.100*** (0.000)	-0.056*** (0.004)	-0.001 (0.176)	-2.36-04 (0.269)	-5.50-04 (0.237)	-9.49-04 (0.190)
REGINDUSTRY	-1.73-04 (0.999)	0.685** (0.038)	0.370* (0.092)	0.031** (0.000)	0.006*** (0.000)	0.008*** (0.002)	0.012*** (0.000)
LAWORIGIN	-0.308 (0.130)	-0.409 (0.399)	-0.322 (0.298)	-0.032*** (0.002)	-0.004** (0.025)	-0.008*** (0.001)	-0.017** (0.016)
LSIZE	-1.984*** (0.000)	-2.260 (0.276)	-2.170*** (0.004)	0.014 (0.639)	-0.003 (0.729)	-0.007 (0.737)	-0.008 (0.679)
POSTPRIVAT	1.011 (0.330)	-4.264*** (0.007)	-0.412 (0.284)	-0.061 (0.190)	-0.007 (0.543)	-0.020 (0.453)	-0.039 (0.235)
Wald $\chi 2$	26.33***	5.04***	48.29***	54.57***	35.59***	24.18***	29.69***
No. of observations	652	652	652	652	652	652	652
No. of groups	75	75	75	75	75	75	75
Hausman	6.82	13.18**	7.29	0.62	1.00	1.13	2.32
R-Squared	0.060	0.031	0.040	0.053	0.033	0.030	0.014

Panel B: First stage of privatisations

Variable	Reg. 2 (ROA)	Reg. 2 (ROE)	Reg. 3 (ROS)	Reg. 4 (SALES/EMP)	Reg. 5 (NP/EMP)	Reg. 6 (OP/EMP)	Reg. 7 (AV/EMP)
Constant	9.786*** (0.000)	6.621 (0.209)	14.113*** (0.000)	0.363*** (0.000)	0.020 (0.313)	0.056 (0.134)	0.149** (0.037)
STATEOWN	-0.037*** (0.000)	0.030 (0.912)	-0.036** (0.048)	-0.002** (0.017)	-9.98-05 (0.570)	-4.30-04 (0.259)	-6.68-04 (0.230)
REGINDUSTRY	0.014 (0.890)	0.298 (0.237)	0.385* (0.091)	0.041*** (0.000)	0.006*** (0.000)	0.100*** (0.000)	0.015*** (0.000)
LAWORIGIN	-0.012 (0.828)	0.798 (0.678)	-0.179 (0.527)	-0.035*** (0.000)	-0.004** (0.015)	-0.007*** (0.001)	-0.015*** (0.002)
LSIZE	0.002 (0.695)	0.011 (0.405)	0.018*** (0.000)	-4.67-05 (0.660)	1.82-05 (0.451)	5.09-06 (0.921)	1.16-05 (0.872)
POSTPRIVAT	-1.307** (0.046)	-1.279 (0.796)	-1.489 (0.162)	-0.068 (0.194)	-0.002 (0.884)	0.019 (0.507)	-0.036 (0.334)
Wald $\chi 2$	17.52***	7.15	23.95***	87.28***	48.11***	41.83***	59.80***
No. of observations	651	651	651	651	651	651	651
No. of groups	78	78	78	78	78	78	78
Hausman	7.07	5.07	7.96	15.78***	3.53	7.02	1.84
R-Squared	0.040	0.000	0.050	0.100	0.040	0.040	0.028

(P-value) * Statistically significant at the 10% level ** Statistically significant at the 5% level *** Statistically significant at the 1% level.

Conclusion

Privatisation and liberalisation have been important phenomena in Europe since the 1980s. This paper contributes to the debate about the effects of privatisation on firm performance by analysing the change in firm profitability and efficiency after privatisation, and the influence of State control, industry and law as determinants of privatised companies' performance for a sample of six European Union countries (France, Finland, Germany, Spain, Sweden and the United Kingdom).

Contrary to the prevailing thinking and previous empirical evidence reported by various authors for multi-country samples, we find no evidence of significant post-privatisation improvements in firms' profitability (either for the multi-country European sample or for the individual countries' sub-samples). Neither do our results support significant improvement in the efficiency of divested firms, when considering each country individually, although they do suggest significant improvements in such firms' efficiency after privatisation for the multi-country sample. What our results support is the claim that the State's relinquishment of control in firms' capital enhances post-privatisation profitability and efficiency, and that in divested firms belonging to regulated industries and to non-common law countries, increases in profitability and efficiency are also higher. However, and regarding the law origin in particular, we must point out that these results should be taken with caution: more countries should be included in the study and further proxies of the institutional environment, such as shareholder rights, law enforcement and accounting standards, should be considered.

References

Alexandre, H., & Charreaux, G. (2004). Efficiency of French privatisations: A dynamic vision. *Journal of Corporate Finance*, *10*, 467-494.

Antoncic, B., & Hisrich, R. (2003). Privatization, corporate entrepreneurship and performance: Testing a normative model. *Journal of Developmental Entrepreneurship*, *8*(3), 197-218.

Arcas, M.J., & Bachiller, P. (2010). Operating performance of privatised firms in Europe: Organizational and environmental factors. *International Journal of Public Administration*, *33*, 487-498.

Argimon, I., Artola, C., & González-Páramo, J. (1999). Empresa pública y privada: Titularidad y eficiencia relativa. *Moneda y Crédito*, *209*, 45-93.

Arocena, P., & Oliveros, D. (2012). The efficiency of state-owned and privatized firms: Does ownership make a difference? *International Journal Production Economics*, *140*, 457-465.

Ausseneg. W., & Jelic, R. (2007). The operating performance of newly privatised firms in Central European transition economies. *European Financial Management*, *13*(5), 853-880.

Bishop, M., & Thomson, D. (1992). Regulatory reform and productivity growth in the UK public utilities. *Applied Economics*, *24*, 1181-1190.

Boardman, A., Claude, L., & Vining, A. (2002). Privatization in Canada: Operating, financial and stock price performance with international comparisons. *Canadian Journal of Administrative Sciences*, *19*(2), 137-157.

Borisova, G., & Megginson, W. (2011). Does government ownership affect the cost of debt? Evidence from privatisation. *The Review of Financial Studies*, *24*(8), 2963-2737.

Bortolotti, B., & Faccio, M. (2009). Government control of privatized firms. *The Review of Financial Studies*, *22*(8), 2907-2938.

Boubakri, N., & Cosset, J. (1998). The financial and operating performance of newly privatized firms: Evidence from developing countries. *The Journal of Finance*, *53*(3), 1081-1110.

Boubakri, N., Cosset, J., & Guedhami, O. (2005a). Liberalization, corporate governance and the performance of privatized firms in developing countries. *Journal of Corporate Finance*, *11*(5), 767-790.

Boubakri, N., Cosset, J., & Guedhami, O. (2005b). Post privatization corporate governance: The role of ownership structure and investor protection. *Journal of Financial Economics*, *76*(2), 369-399.

Boubakri, N., Cosset, J.-C., Guedhami, O., & Saffar, W. (2011). The political economy of residual state ownership in privatized firms: Evidence from emerging markets. *Journal of Corporate Finance*, *17*, 244-258.

Boubakri, N., Cosset, J., & Saffar, W. (2015). The constraints on full privatization: International evidence. *Journal of Corporate Finance*, in press.

Boycko, M., Shleifer, A., & Vishny, R. (1993). Privatisating Russia. *Brookings Papers on Economic Activity*, *2*, 81-139.

Boycko, M., Sheilfer, A., & Visnhy, R. (1996). A theory of privatization. *The Economic Journal*, *106*(1), 327-377.

Brown, D., Earle, J., & Telegdy, A. (2010). Employment and wage effects on privatisation: Evidence from Hungary, Romania, Russia and Ukraine. *The Economic Journal*, *120*, 683-708.

Brown, J., Earle, J., & Telegdy, A. (2006). The productivity effects of privatization: Longitudinal estimates from Hungary, Romania, Russia and Ukraine. *Journal of Political Economy*, *114*(1), 61-99.

Cabeza-García, L., & Gómez-Ansón, S. (2012). What drives the operating performance of privatised firms? *Scottish Journal of Political Economy*, *59*(1), 1-27.

Claessens, S., Djankov, G., & Pohl, D. (1997). Ownership structure and corporate performance: Evidence from the Czech Republic. Working Paper 1737, World Bank Policy Research.

Claessens, S., & Djankov, S. (2002). Privatization benefits in Eastern Europe. *Journal of Public Economics*, *83*, 307-324.

Cuervo, A., & Maroto, J. (1983). Análisis económico-financiero comparativo entre grandes empresas industriales públicas y privadas. Años 1979-80 y 1980-81. *Economía Industrial*, 231, 49-72.

Cuervo, A. (1997). *La privatización de la empresa pública*. Madrid: Ediciones Encuentro.

De Alessi, L. (1980). The economics of property rights: A review of the evidence. *Research in Law and Economics*, *2*, 1-47.

Denisova, I., Eller, M., Frye, T., & Zhurasvkaya, E. (2012). Everybody hates privatisation, but why? Survey evidence from 28 post-communist countries. *Journal of Comparative Economics*, *40*, 44-61.

Dewenter, K., & Malatesta, P. (2001). State-owned and privately-owned firms: An empirical analysis of profitability, leverage and labour intensity. *American Economic Review*, *91*, 320-334.

Djankov, S., & Murell, P. (2002). Enterprise restructuring in transition: A quantitative survey. *Journal of Economic Literature*, *40*(3), 739-792.

D'Souza, J., & Megginson, W. (1999). The financial and operating performance of privatized firms during the 1990s. *The Journal of Finance*, *54*(4), 1397-1437.

D'Souza, J., Megginson, W., & Nash, R. (2005). Effect of institutional and firm specific characteristics on post-privatization performance: Evidence from developed countries. *Journal of Corporate Finance*, *11*(5), 747-766.

D'Souza, J., Megginson, W., & Nash, R. (2007). The effects of changes in corporate governance and restructurings on operating performance: Evidence from privatisations. *Global Finance Journal*, *18*, 157-184.

Ehrlich, I., Gallais-Hamonno, G., Zhiqiang L., & Lutter, R. (1994). Productivity growth and firm ownership: An empirical investigation. *Journal of Political Economics*, *102*, 1006-1038.

Estrin, S., Hanousek, J., Kocena, E., & Svejnar, J. (2009). The effect of privatization and ownership in transition economies. *Journal of Economic Literature*, *473*, 699-728.

Faccio, M. (2010). Differences between politically connected firms and non-connected firms: A cross country analysis. *Financial Management*, *autumn*, 905-927.

Frydman, R., Gray, Ch., Hessel, M., & Rapaczynski, A. (2000). The limits of discipline: Ownership and hard budget constraints in the transition economies. *The Economics of Transition*, *8*(3), 577-603.

González-Páramo, J. M. (1995). Privatización y eficiencia. ¿Es irrelevante la titularidad? *Economistas*, *63*, 32-43.

Grosse, R., &Yanes, J. (1998). Carrying out a successful privatization: The YPF case. *Academy Management Executive*, *12*, 64-73.

Harper, J. (2002). The performance of privatized firms in the Czech Republic. *Journal of Banking and Finance*, *26*, 621-649.

Hausman, J. (1978). Specification test in economics. *Econométrica*, *46*, 1251-1271.

Hausman, J., & Taylor, W. (1981). Panel data and unobservable individual effects. *Econométrica*, *49*(6), 1377-1398.

La Porta, R., López de Silanes F., Sheilfer, A., & Visnhy, R. (1997). Legal determinants of external finance. *The Journal of Finance*, *52*(3), 1131-1150.

La Porta, R., López de Silanes F., Sheilfer, A., & Visnhy, R. (1998). Law and Finance. *Journal of Political Economics*, *106*, 1113-1150.

La Porta, R., & López de Silanes, F. (1999). The benefits of privatisation: Evidence from Mexico. *Quarterly Journal of Economics*, *November*, 1193-1242.

La Porta, R., Lopez de Silanes, F., & Shleifer, A. (2008). The economic consequences of legal origins. *Journal of Economic Literature*, *16*(2), 285-332.

Laffont, J., & Tirole, J. (1993). *A theory of incentives in procurement and regulation*. Cambridge: The MIT Press.

Li, W., & Xu, L. (2004). The impact of privatization and competition in the telecommunications sector around the world. *The Journal of Law and Economics*, *57*, 395-431.

Marcelin, I., & Mathur, I. (2015). Privatization, financial development, property rights and growth. *Journal of Banking & Finance*, *50*, 528-546.

Martin, S., & Parker, D. (1995). Privatization and economic performance throughout the UK Business Cycle. *Managerial and Decision Economics*, *16*, 225-237.

Megginson, W., & Netter, J. (2001). From State to market: A survey of empirical studies on privatization. *Journal of Economic Literature*, *39*, 321-389.

Megginson, W., Nash, R., & Van Randerborgh, M. (1994). The financial and operating performance of newly privatized firms: An international analysis. *The Journal of Finance*, *49*, 403-452.

Ng, C., & Seabright, P. (2001). Competition, privatisation and productive efficiency: Evidence from the airlines industry. *The Economic Journal*, *111*, 591-629.

Pagano, M., & Roell, A. (1998). The choice of stock ownership structure: Agency cost, monitoring and the decision to go public. *Quarterly Journal of Economics*, *113*(1), 187-225.

Pestieau, P., & Tulkens, H. (1993). Assessing and explaining the performance of public enterprises. *Finanzarchiv*, *50*, 293-323.

Privatization Barometer (2014). http://www.privatizationbarometer.net/PUB/NL/5/3/PB_AR2013-2014.pdf.

Reeves, E., & Placic, D. (2004). Privatization policy and enterprise performance: The case of Ireland. *Annals of Public and Cooperative Economics*, *75*(4), 525-548.

Sheshinski, E., & López-Calva, L. (2003). Privatization and its benefits: Theory and evidence. *CESifo Economics Studies*, *49*(3), 429-459.

Shirley, M., & Nellis, J. (1991). Public enterprise reform. The lessons of experience. World Bank, Economic development Institute, Washington DC.

Shleilfer, A., & Vinshy, R. (1996). A theory of privatization. *The Economic Journal*, *106*, 309-319.

Sun, Q., & Tong, W. (2003). China share issue privatization: The extent of its success. *Journal of Financial Economics*, *70*, 183-222.

Vickers, J., & Yarrow, G. (1988). *Privatization. An economic analysis.* Cambridge: The MIT Press.

Villalonga, B. (2000). Privatization and efficiency: Differentiating ownership effects from political, organizational and dynamics effects. *Journal of Economic Behaviour & Organization*, *42*, 43-74.

Vining, A., & Boardam, A. (1992). Ownership versus competition: Efficiency in public enterprise. *Public Choice*, *73*, 205-239.

Wei, Z., Varela, O., D'Souza, J., & Kabir, H. (2003). The financial and operating performance of China's newly privatized firms. *Financial Management*, *summer*, 107-126.

Yarrow, G. (1986). Privatization in theory and practice. *Economic Policy*, *2*, 324-377.

Yarrow, G. (1989). Privatization and economic performance in Britain. Carnegie Rochester Series on Public Policy, no. 3.

Biographical Sketches

Laura Cabeza-García

Name: Laura Cabeza-García
Affiliation: University of León
Date of Birth: 07/03/1979
Education: BA in Business Administration, PhD. Economics
Address: Facultad de C.C. Económicas y Empresariales,
Campus de Vegazana s/n, 24071 León

Research and Professional Experience: Privatisations, Corporate Governance, Corporate Social Responsibility

Professional Appointments: Present (since 2012): Associate Professor at University of León (Spain)
Assistant Professor at University of León (2005-2012)
Assistant Professor at University of Oviedo (2005)

Honors:

Publications Last 3 Years:

- Martínez-Campillo, A.; **Cabeza-García, L.**; Marbella-Sánchez, F. (2013). "Responsabilidad social corporativa y resultado financiero: Evidencia sobre la doble dirección de la causalidad en el sector de las cajas de ahorros." *Cuadernos de Dirección y Economía de la Empresa*, 13(1), pp. 54-68. [**JCR Impact factor (2013):** 0,286;

Business (Q4: 100/111)]. [**JCR Impact factor (2014):** 0,293; Business (Q4: 105/115)]

- Testera, A. and **Cabeza, L.** (2013). "Análisis de los factores determinantes de la transparencia en RSC en las empresas españolas cotizadas." *Intangible Capital*, 9(1), pp. 225-261. [Scopus]
- **Cabeza, L.;** Fernández, R.; Matilla, L. (2013). "Análisis de los determinantes de la transparencia en RSC desde la perspectiva del buen gobierno." *Ekonomiaz: Revista Vasca de Economía*, 83(2), pp. 273-296. [Econlit, Catálogo de Latindex].
- **Cabeza, L.** (2014). "Responsabilidad social y gobierno corporativo", en Vázquez, J.L., Licandro, O. & Lanero, A. (Eds.): *Perspectivas en el estudio de la Responsabilidad Social Corporativa. Aplicaciones Prácticas en Uruguay y España*, pp. 131-146, Grupo Magro Editores.
- **Cabeza, L.**; Sacristán, M.; Gómez, S. (2014). "Propiedad familiar, control y efecto generación y RSC." *Revista de Empresa Familiar*, 4(1), pp. 9-22. [Catálogo de Latindex].
- Godos-Díez, J.L.; Fernández-Gago, R.; **Cabeza-García, L.**; Martínez-Campillo, A. (2014). "Determinants of CSR practices: Analysis of the influence of ownership and the management profile mediating effect." *Spanish Journal of Finance and Accounting*, 43(1), pp. 47-90. [**JCR impact factor (2014):** 0,220; Business, Finance (Q4: 85/88)].
- Sacristán-Navarro, M.; Gómez-Ansón, S.; **Cabeza-García, L.** (2014). "Other large shareholders in families firms: do they monitor?", en Smyrnios, K., Panikkos, P. & Goel, S. (Eds.): "2nd. Handbook of Research on family firms," capítulo 8, pp. 161-183, Edward Elgar Publishers. [Included in Book Citation Index; Web of Science; Thomson Reuters].
- Godos-Díez, J.L; Fernández-Gago, R.; **Cabeza-García, L.** (2015). "Business education and idealism as determinants of stakeholder orientation." *Journal of Business Ethics*, 131(2), pp. 439-452. [**JCR impact factor (2014):** 1,326; Ethics (Q1: 8/552) Business (Q3: 60/115)].
- Godos-Díez, J.L.; Fernández-Gago, R.; **Cabeza-García, L.** (2015). "Normative stakeholder management orientation: Business vs. Non-business students." *Society & Economy*, 37(4), pp. 477-492 [Scopus]
- Sacristán-Navarro, M.; **Cabeza-García, L.**; Gómez-Ansón, S. (2015). "The company you keep: The effect of other large shareholders in

family firms." *Corporate Governance: An International Review*, 23(3), pp. 216-233. [**JCR impact factor (2014): 1,734;** Business, Finance (Q1: 12/88) Business (Q2: 42/115) Management (Q2: 62/185)].
- Fernández-Gago, R.; **Cabeza-García, L.**; Nieto, M. (2016). "Corporate social responsibility, board of directors, and firm performance: an analysis of their relationships." *Review of Managerial Science*, 10, pp. 85-104. [**JCR Impact factor (2014):** 0,857; Management (Q3: 124/185)].

Sonia Medina-Salgado

Name: Sonia Medina-Salgado
Affiliation: Universidad Rey Juan Carlos
Date of Birth: 03/10/1969
Education: BA Economic and Business Administration, PhD. Economics
Address: P° Artilleros s/n, 28032 Madrid, Spain

Research and Professional Experience: Corporate governance, Strategy and Management of information technology.

Professional Appointments: Controller at Groupama from 1994 to 1996. Associate Professor at European University from 1996 to 2000. Associate Professor at Rey Juan Carlos University Madrid, since 2004.

Honors:

Publications Last 3 Years:

- García-Muiña, F.E.; González-Sánchez, R.; **Medina-Salgado, S.** (2014). "El modelo de negocio como brújula en entornos dinámicos: el caso de Amadeus." *Dirección y Organización*, 54, 3-20. [Catálogo de Latindex, Scopus].
- Ortelt, S.; **Medina-Salgado, S.** (2014). "La importancia de las políticas socialmente responsables de las empresas turísticas españolas. una revisión de iniciativas e índices." *Turydes*, 7(16). [Catálogo de Latindex, InRecs].

María Sacristán-Navarro

Name: María Sacristán-Navarro
Affiliation: Universidad Rey Juan Carlos
Date of Birth: 25/10/1968
Education: BA Business Administration, PhD. Economics
Address: Pº Artilleros s/n, 28032 Madrid, Spain

Research and Professional Experience: Research experience on corporate governance, family firms and strategy.
Professional Appointments: At Rey Juan Carlos University, Associate Professor of Strategy, Department of Business Administration (Administración, Dirección y Organización), Rey Juan Carlos University, Madrid, since 2001. PHD Program (*Research on Family Business*), Rey Juan Carlos University, Madrid.

Honors: Scholarship Fundación Rafael del Pino para Jóvenes Talentos, 2014.
Prize Alden G. Lank & FBCG Award, 2004 to the best communication given by the Family Business Network in the XV World Congress FBN-IFERA.

Publications Last 3 Years:

- Cabeza, L.; **Sacristán, M.**; Gómez, S. (2014). "Propiedad familiar, control y efecto generación y RSC." *Revista de Empresa Familiar*, 4(1), pp. 9-20. [Catálogo de Latindex].
- **Sacristán-Navarro, M.**; Gómez-Ansón, S.; Cabeza-García, L. (2014). "Other large shareholders in family firms: do they monitor?", con M. Sacristán y L. Cabeza, en *2nd. Handbook of Research on Family Business,* eds. Poutziouris, P.Z.; Smyrnios, K.X.; Goel, S., Edward Elgar Publishing. [Included in Book Citation Index; Web of Science; Thomson Reuters].
- **Sacristán-Navarro, M.**; Cabeza-García, L.; Gómez-Ansón, S. (2015). "The company you keep: The effect of other large shareholders in family firms." *Corporate Governance: An International Review*, 23(3), pp. 216-233. [**JCR impact factor (2014): 1,734;** Business, Finance (Q1: 12/88) Business (Q2: 42/115) Management (Q2: 62/185)].

Silvia Gómez-Ansón

Name: Silvia Gómez-Ansón
Affiliation: University of Oviedo
Date of Birth: 06/03/1967
Education: BA in Economics and Business Administration, Master in International Economics, PhD in Economics and Business Administration
Address: Departamento de Administración de Empresas, Facultad de Ciencias Económicas y Empresariales, Universidad de Oviedo, Avda. del Cristo s/n, Oviedo 33007

Research and Professional Experience: Corporate Finance, Privatisations, Corporate Governance, Family firms, Corporate Social Responsibility

Professional Appointments: Present: Professor of Finance and Accounting, University of Oviedo, Spain.
Formerly Visiting Professor at the Faculty of Economics of the Otto-von-Guericke Universität Magdeburg, the Faculty of Economics and Business Administration of the Europa Universität Viadrina and the University of Torino.

Publications Last 3 Years:

- Cabeza, L.; Sacristán, M.; **Gómez, S.** (2014). "Propiedad familiar, control y efecto generación y RSC." *Revista de Empresa Familiar*, 4(1), pp. 9-20. [Catálogo de Latindex].
- Sacristán-Navarro, M.; **Gómez-Ansón, S**.; Cabeza-García, L. (2014). "Other large shareholders in family firms: do they monitor?", con M. Sacristán y L. Cabeza, en *2nd. Handbook of Research on Family Business,* eds. Poutziouris, P.Z.; Smyrnios, K.X.; Goel, S., Edward Elgar Publishing. [Included in Book Citation Index; Web of Science; Thomson Reuters].
- Sacristán-Navarro, M.; Cabeza-García, L.; **Gómez-Ansón, S.** (2015). "The company you keep: The effect of other large shareholders in family firms." *Corporate Governance: An International Review*, 23(3), pp. 216-233. [**JCR impact factor (2014): 1,734;** Business, Finance (Q1: 12/88) Business (Q2: 42/115) Management (Q2: 62/185)].

In: Privatization
Editor: Amelia Hansen
ISBN: 978-1-63484-749-0
© 2016 Nova Science Publishers, Inc.

Chapter 3

THE CHALLENGES OF CONSERVATION AND LARGE-SCALE AGRICULTURAL DEVELOPMENT IN AN ERA OF NEOLIBERAL ENVIRONMENTAL GOVERNANCE IN CAMEROON

Ngambouk Vitalis Pemunta
Centre for Concurrences in Colonial and Postcolonial Studies,
Linnaeus University, Växjo, Sweden

ABSTRACT

The adoption of Western imposed neoliberal development policies by most African countries has resulted in unfettered effects. Through these policies, Western-based development institutions (the World Bank and the International Monetary Fund) have subsequently come to have a lot of leverage on development policies and practices in the donor dependent countries of the Less Developed world including Cameroon. In Cameroon, one area of neoliberal governmentality involves the management of the environment which is at crossroads with the establishment of largescale agricultural plantations by Western multinationals operating in the country. This paper explores how the American-based agro-industrial company Herakles Farm has thoroughly disregarded state and international laws and codes of conduct in the setting up of its contentious oil palm plantation that is largely located in between protected areas in the ever-green forest of Southwest Cameroon. Through its creation of uninhabited spaces via protected areas in the region, and by its ceding of land around these same protected areas for large-scale agricultural development, the state of Cameroon is involved in the reordering of the man-nature relationship. The state's action bespeaks of the chasm between conservation and large-scale agricultural development in an era of neoliberal environmental governance. The paper argues that the Herakle concession is a means by which the state is territorializing and controlling this unruly frontier space. It is also representative of a long trajectory of the marginalization of this space that has been discursively produced over and over and that allows for dispossession and accumulation in the name of development. The state's creation of developmentalizable and governable spaces has disrupted local livelihoods in a region that has been consistently touted as a frontier space by both colonial and postcolonial powers.

Keywords: neoliberalism, neoliberal governmentality, conservation, development, frontier, Herakles Farm, agricultural development, conservation and development, environmental governance

INTRODUCTION

The neoliberal quest for large swathes of arable land for agricultural development to feed populations and for the supply of biofuels for foreign markets has led to the creation of frontiers as multinationals compete for land (and other natural resources) in the global South (Pemunta 2014). One of several foreign actors involved in large-scale land grabbing in Cameroon is American-based Herakles Farms. This agro-industrial consortium is setting up a palm oil plantation sandwiched in the protected areas of the evergreen forest of Southwest Cameroon in total disregard of both national and international laws governing foreign direct investments. The government of Cameroon (GoC) is simultaneously involved in the production of territory through the creation of uninhabited spaces including protected areas and national parks and in the re-ordering of human-nature relationships. The state is also concurrently involved in the provisioning of a facilitative regime to capitalist development as a way of linking itself to the circuit of global capitalism. By concurrently authorizing large-scale agricultural development and conservation, the state has put itself at the cross-roots between development and neoliberal conservation in an area that has consistently been considered a "no-man's land."

Drawing on the concept of frontier, this paper demonstrates that through the Cameroon government's simultaneous creation of developmentalizable entities and territorialization practices operationalized through the creation of protected areas, people are presented as standing in the way of neoliberal "progress" and development. This is encapsulated by the Herakles farm plantation that has become synonymous with underdevelopment in the Ndian and Koupe-Manengouba Divisions of Southwest Cameroon. How has Herakles been so thoroughly successful in violating both national and international environmental standards? What mechanisms allowed for this to happen? What are the consequences on small-holder farmers?

Among the litany of violations of both national and international laws are unlawful and unilateral demarcation of land without prior, informed consent, a flawed environmental and social impact assessment report (ESAI), the illegal felling of trees and timber exploitation, outright disrespect of restraining court orders, negative environmental consequences on soils, increased migration and depletion of resources, the suppression of forest resources as well as the displacement of the local population.

The Frontier, Territorialization and Neoliberalism

A frontier can be defined as "an area over which political control by the regional metropoles is absent or uncertain" (Kopytoff 1987b:170). It is essentially a politically constructed space: "the frontier is above all a political fact, a matter of political definition of geographical space" (Ibid 1987a:11). The frontier logic is characterized by a triple, complementary and partly distinctive political dimension: (1) an ideological project or an imaginary construction by those making claims over political space at the margins of the metropole. The frontier is therefore constructed as a political vacuum or a "no man's land" that needs to be claimed or occupied by outsiders: 'the frontier as an institutional vacuum' as "the metropole [defining] an area in its periphery as open to legitimate intrusion" (Kopytoff, 1987a:9,16). Secondly, it is a geographical space where state power is territorialized through material and symbolic mechanisms. The state divides peripheral territories into "complex and overlapping political and economic zones and rearranges people and resources within these units, and create(s) regulations delineating how and by whom these areas can be used" (Vandergeest and Peluso, 1995:387).

Governmentality is ensured through population movements, public policies, property right regimes, and variegated center-periphery relations. Thirdly, the frontier is characterized by disorder and violence of a contradictory nature. It is a contact zone between settler and indigenous populations, different cultural styles, a meeting point of nationally defined territories where the metropole regulates the hinterland using territorial strategies.

Under neoliberalism, territorialization has assumed three dimensions. First, it involves a synergy between state and non-state institutions in environmental governance. As state 'territories' protected areas are developed and managed by a network of alliances comprised of state, private and not-for profit-largely transnational entities. This might be referred to as 'internal territorialization' (Vandergeest and Peluso, 1995:385) or 'internal colonialism.' Secondly, territorialization entails "both a claim to control land and resources as well as a claim to authority so as to determine control over those resources." Through their participation in the design and subsequent implementation of protected area governance mechanisms, transnational actor's "[legitimize] their claims both to forest lands themselves and to the authority to determine forest policy." The process of governance involves how decisions get made and implemented and is intricately intertwined with legitimacy. Thirdly, through practices of enclosure, these network of actors do not only stake claims on rural peasant's lands, but are also entitled to the authority to determine, who can accumulate from them and under what circumstances. They tend to consolidate non-state and foreign access to the process of determining land and resource rights, and thus the accumulation of wealth (Corson, 2011:705).

This paper argues that the Herakles Farm concession is a means by the state of Cameroon to territorialize and control the unruly frontier areas of the Ndian and KupeManenguba Divisions of Southwest Cameroon. While it is representative of a long trajectory of the marginalization of this space that has been discursively produced over time and that allows for dispossession and marginalization, non-state actors particularly conservation NGOs and foreign aid donors were instrumental in this territorialization process. These stakeholders linked neoliberalism with sustainable development through the spatial reordering practice of protected areas and national parks. This process of neoliberal state territorialization is happening in a context where the state, borrowing its cue from the colonial land tenure and Eurocentric developmentalist template has turned local communities into "virtual land owners and tenants" who could be evicted at any time and without consultation in the name of "development" (Pemunta, 2013). In other words, the state produces space (see Brenner, 2001, Brenner and Elden, 2009) and subsequently the reordering of nature (Pemunta, 2013). The paper points to the difficulties of simultaneous compliance with neoliberal market reforms in a neoliberal era of environmental conservation.

This paper is based on multi-sited ethnography (Marcus, 1995) and embedded in a dual case study-a Cameroonian and a subnational case study of land grabbing that exposes state-supported violence. It articulates the complexity between the role of the state and violence in Southwest Cameroon. The data collection process involved movement across various villages (sites) affected by the Herakles oil palm plantation, while conducting in-depth interviews, formal and informal discussion sessions and participant observation with stakeholders. This multilocale methodological framework helped in "contextualization through macro-constructions of a larger social order, such as the capitalist world system, to multiple sites of observation and participation that cross-cut dichotomies such as the "local" and the "global," the "life world" and the "system" (Marcus, 1995:95). These methodological approaches are complemented by published reports from national and international civil society actors, think tanks and academic institutions that have written on, and are largely opposed to the project because of Herakles total disregard for environmental and social concerns. This alliance of transnational actors has also deplored the troublesome role of the state of Cameroon-transnational agro-alliance that is embedded in the state's neoliberal policies, spatial practices and narratives of representation that facilitate large-scale agribusiness. These policies include the state's monopoly over land and natural resources (see also Pemunta 2014). While this is an assertion of the supremacy of legal over customary land tenure rights, the state further enforces its authority through its production of territory. At the same time, a conjuncture between the state's lack of "statehardness": weak laws and the lack of enforcement mechanisms as well as corruption have extinguished customary land rights thereby leaving local communities as "virtual land owners and tenants" (Pemunta, 2013).

THE POLITICS OF DEVELOPMENT: "VIRTUAL LANDLORDS AND TENANTS"

Cameroon was, and continues to be inordinately affected by a conjuncture between multiple shifts in the global economy and the policies of multilateral donors such as the World Bank and the International Monetary Fund (IMF). These multilateral donors pushed for the imposition of the Structural Adjustment Programme (SAP) and the notion of conservation and development on the country in the 1990s. Apart from imposing the privatization of state-owned enterprises and the liberalization of the economy, they simultaneously shaped "state territorialization under neoliberalism" (Corson 2011) through the creation of national parks and protected areas. This process involved non-state (foreign aid donors, international non-governmental conservation organizations, (INGCOs)) as well as state actors (agencies, branches and levels of state) thereby challenging notions of state territorialization [practices] as a state controlled process. The state is simply a vehicle through which myriad non-state actors "sought to expand their control of and authority over…forests" (Corson 2011:703) for private capital accumulation in the name of biodiversity conservation. The adoption of neoliberalism was happening against the backdrop of a drastic fall in the value of agricultural products in the world market. This price volatility in the international market was further accompanied by the devaluation of the francs CFA in 1994 and widespread poverty that was most magnified among the rural masses, most of whom depend on subsistence agriculture. Eager to jump start its moribund economy and to link the country to the circuit of global capitalism, the country's leadership has been keen on attracting foreign direct investment, but reforms-particularly land reforms lag behind. Apart from the unilateral imposition of market-oriented economic reforms throughout Africa in the 1990s, these bilateral and multilateral development actors also linked conservation and sustainable development. This implied the expansion or creation of protected areas and national parks which is a form of territorialization that excludes rural farmers from arable land and associated timber and non-timber forest products (NTFPs) for the benefit of the "global commons" (see also Corson, 2011:704, Kelly 2011:683).

After more than three decades and counting in power, the Paul Biya led autocratic regime finally formulated a Long-term Vision for the Development of Cameroon with the aim of providing an image of the country by 2035 so as to transform it into.".. an emerging, democratic and united" nation in its diversity (African Development Bank, 2009:1). Code named "Greater Ambition," this vision is to be achieved through a series of grandiose infrastructural projects: hydroelectric and energy plants, telecommunication networks, mining, urbanization, industrialization, state-led housing schemes for the "poor," transport and communication and the expansion of the agricultural sector through large-scale agribusiness with foreign funding or by foreign investors who have been invited into the country and given mouth-watering generous tax concessions so as to help with Cameroon's insertion into the international market. These projects have witnessed outright violations of both national and international law on the management of the environment and on standard international business practices, and are likely to exacerbate food insecurity and environmental degradation (see also Pemunta 2014). For example, although the government's Rural Sector Development Plan proposes to raise palm oil production to 300,000 (2015) and 450,000 tons (2020), these targets are to be achieved mainly by increasing oil production yields and the area under oil palm production as well as by increasing oil extraction rates. The plan is focused on the area under production targets, but neither on yields nor on any environmental or biodiversity impacts (Hoyle and Levang, 2012:5). However, new investments in forest areas, such as oil palm plantations, oil and mineral extraction, and infrastructure and energy projects are likely to increase forest loss. While this developmentalist vision is clearly an assertion of narratives of inclusive national development (Gupta and Ferguson 2002, see also Martinez, 2011:38), that seek to legitimize processes of forced displacement and dispossession, it is being implemented in sharp contradiction to neither any redistributive attempts at land reforms nor an institutional reorientation that recognizes community land tenure and ownership so as to deliver on climate change calls, conservation and to improve livelihoods. These are the very kernel of any meaningful socioeconomic development. Within this framework, the political class has annexed isolated regional areas and economies including the evergreen forests of the Ndian and Kupemuanenguba Divisions of Southwest Cameroon-the sites of the Herakles plantation- to articulate a national project combining capital, technology, and market schemes to ensure the region's access to 'quick fix development.' Cameroon's Growth and Employment Strategy Paper (GESP) which is anchored on, and a mechanism for the operationalization of this vision as well as for the achievement of the Millennium Development Goals (MDGs) seeks to do away with the factors that stymied the judicious management of state property by, among others-lifting the land constraint so as to facilitate the development of communication infrastructure, and promoting the opening up of small- and large-scale farms in the rural sector (Government of Cameroon, 2009, African Development Bank, 2009).

TERRITORIALIZATION AND THE SUBORDINATION OF SMALL-HOLDER FARMERS IN CAMEROON

This section examines the long history of the creation of territory and the subordination of small-holder land resource and tenure to international and national economic goals including resource appropriation through plantation agriculture and biodiversity conservation by colonial and postcolonial powers.

In Cameroon, the subordination of small-holder´s land and natural resources through the notion of territory and territorialization began with the German colonial power, continued with the dual British and French colonial regimes into the postcolonial state. Simultaneously, Cameroon's forest resources are also characterized by a long history of regulatory and institutional settings. During the colonial period, Germany, the United Kingdom, and France had administrative units in place to regulate the forestry sector (Hédin 1930, Letouzey 1957). In their territorialization policy, these powers asserted the primacy of written over customary land tenure which was an indirect assertion of the colonial state's monopoly over land and other natural resources at the detriment of smallholder farmers. Communal land ownership was supplanted by individual land ownership and land was commodified since "colonial authorities forcefully contended that the communal ownership of land (or any property for that matter) was antithetical to the principal tenets of capitalism." They accordingly instituted a dual system of land ownership: the traditional system for native Africans, "…the 'modern' system for Europeans and the few Europeanized members of the native population." Apart from the nationalization of natural resources, large tracts of land were set aside for conservation and resources such as wildlife was put under a central regulatory authority, thereby extinguishing local people's resource use rights. The colonial masters initially undertook large-scale reforestation schemes through the planting of thousands of exotic and native timber species. They later adopted a totally protectionist policy because of widespread clearance for farming and to a lesser extent, logging. The dominant orthodox view of overwhelming and rapid deforestation became the institutionalized policy framework within West African administration and policies (Fairhead and Leach, 1998:168, cf Pemunta and Mbu-Arrey, 2013:7). Africans were herded into unproductive land and their chances of accessing land in the desirable areas was nullified (Njoh, 2008:91, Njoh, 2009:304). The colonial masters began the process of territorialization through the spatial delimitation of land by creating 'white only enclaves' and the putting in place of rules as to the use of land as well as who can use it. Control over land was a mechanism of controlling economic resources as well as a significant indicator of power. All owners of land had to be identified and registered in the German land register (*Grundbuch*) and ownership was reckoned in terms of "effective occupation" through plantation agriculture which the Germans introduced in the Southwest region. As Njoh maintains "[T]he land register was also a critical element in the colonial state's effort to bolster its power through the acquisition and control of vital data. Above all, the formalization of all transactions in land through the bureaucratic apparatus and the concomitant defrayment of fees and other charges guaranteed the colonial state a steady source of revenue that would otherwise not be available at its disposal. The colonial state's control of land use activities guaranteed it further revenue from real estate taxes (e.g., the hut tax of the British colonial territories), building permit fees, surveyor's fees and so on" (Njoh, 2009:309). Like the Germans, the French considered "primary forests" as not being in use and "…primarily as forests in which the local people have never exercised any right….. They were undoubtedly of the character of forest empty and without owners" (*vacantes et sans maître*) (Auberville, 1949:100, Fairhead and Leach, 1998:169). Although the British recognized native land rights, such lands were however under the control of the colonial state.

In former British Cameroon, large tracts of native land were carved out as "virgin forest," as land reserves-with the covert aim of either logging them or appropriating same for agriculture (Mayers and Bass, 1998:276). Reserves were also created for the protection of watersheds, as shelter belts (Martin, 1991:18) as well as for the maintenance of climatic conditions favourable for agric production (Parren and de Graaj, 1995:41). Africans were accused of being unable to manage human-nature relationship. They were "accused of 'abusing' nature in ways that would lead to the possible extinction of game and the disruption of monuments of nature." Furthermore, Europeans linked discourses of conservation and colonial sovereignty to create national parks (Dunn, 2009:436). The Southwest region is not only part of the West African "cocoa belt," it has been the site of plantation agriculture (rubber, tea and bananas) in general and palm oil production in particular for colonial and postcolonial powers. This thus implies the region's longstanding linkage to the global economy as well as its simultaneous subjugation to the production of local and international spaces. Conservation as an act of governmentality upon this region, its people and their natural resources erased traditional usage rights. Territorialized areas, Igoe and Brockington (2007:441) concede are 'transnationalised spaces, governed according to the needs and agendas of transnational networks of actors and institutions.' These networks negotiate resource use rights and access at multiple scales. The emergence of conservation advocates in battles over land and natural resources has resonances to colonialism and is a reinforcement of broader political and economic structures that have 'historically marginalized rural peasants from the sources of their livelihoods'(Corson 2011:707).

The German colonial administration forcefully appropriated local labour for the establishment of local colonial infrastructures: roads, railways and plantations which served as incentives to the colonial enterprise. Furthermore, land was also used to reward cronies and agents of colonialism. Parcels of land were either awarded free of charge or at token prices to European settler farmers and miners. This act of double dispossession granted colonial agents unfettered access to both land and other natural resources as well as to local sources of labour. "The mass appropriation of lands on the part of the state as a means of reinforcing its economic prowess, thereby, consolidating its political power, occurred throughout colonial Africa." In Cameroon for instance, using the threat of military force, most of the fertile volcanic lands at the foot of Mount Cameroon was unilaterally transferred to European plantation farmers and the indigenous Bakweri population were herded into reserves and without any compensation (Njoh, 2009:310; Pemunta and Fonmboh, 2010) Indigenous subsistence farmers who had little incentive to engage in wage labour on European plantations were forced by the colonial administration into doing so. Contrary to the Germans, the British abolished forceful labour recruitment. Rather, they recruited workers by offering cash wages, which were in turn used to pay taxes to the colonial state. By providing wages, the British colonial administration attracted many migrants from Southern Cameroon (Le Vine, 1964:196-197). On their part, the French colonial administration re-imposed the German labour tax in a disguised form *prestation*, mostly for railway construction. Harsh labour conditions and the mistreatment of workers eventuated into death rates averaging about 60 per thousand labourers (Le Vine, 1964:104-110, Firmin-Sellers, 2001). Chiefs and colonial officials were complacent and exploited native labour for their personal interests. They used kidnapping alongside corporal punishment to meet up with labour demands and were particularly enthusiastic in enforcement because they were often able to divert labourers for work on private farms and plantations. The worst aspects of the system were rescinded under international pressure in 1930. However, the *prestation* continued in various forms until 1952, and continues to evoke bitter memories among those who lived through it (Rubin 1971:57, Firmin-Sellers, 2001). Despite apparent differences between French and

British colonial rule, they used the local administrative structure for tax collection and labour mobilization. Both further used tax revenue to finance the metropole. While they extracted high revenue; they insisted that their colonies be self-financing. French *corvée* labour was physically brutal. They appropriated native labour to build bridges and railways and to work on European plantations. Labourers were shabbily treated and often returned home crippled and maimed (Firmin-Sellers, 2001:48-49).

The legal dualism instituted by colonial and postcolonial powers- what Mamoud Mamdani (1996) calls institutionalized despotism, remains a hallmark of Cameroon's legal landscape and land tenure system. This situation has generated competing legitimacy claims between local and traditional against modern power structures over land. By working through and appealing to different normative registers with which they are confronted, they at times "reinforce the legitimacy of authorities serving as representatives of these varied state and 'traditional institutions" (Belaunde et al., 2010:5) who then cash in on competing parties to any parcel of land (see Pemunta 2014). Europeans and *evolués* were subjected to the laws of the mother country, while "natives" were subjected to customary law. This law was however, usually interpreted and enforced by the colonial administration. In present-day Cameroon, customary law remains a source of land law and personal law (Anyangwe, 1987: 234). Despite attempts at harmonization, two formally recognized legal systems, the outcome of the Franco-British partition exists in Cameroon: common law (West Cameroon) and civil law in East Cameroon. The former attributes legal standing to judicial opinions and traditions (precedence), while in the latter, decisions are based on codified legal text. Civil law is less solicitous to private property than common law. The former overemphasizes the perceived needs of the public which is a tacit mechanism through which the state has stamped its authority on land and natural resources including forestry against societal authority and control as overall owner. According to the 1974 Ordinance "The state shall be the guardian of all lands. It may in this capacity intervene to ensure rational use of land or in the imperative interest of defense or the economic policies of the nation" (cf Njoh, 2009:310).

The colonial masters tremendously transformed Cameroon's land tenure regime through the introduction of the notion, and subsequently, the triumph of private property over customary rights. This paradigm subsequently erased smallholders from the colonial notion of "development" as evidence of the "effective occupation" of land which was defined in terms of plantation farming. Apart from the unfettered effects of various colonial regimes of governmentality, there is also the coexistence of a traditional or "customary" land tenure system which is in a flux as well as a "modern" land tenure regime which is written, introduced through colonization to promote individual ownership basically by colonialists (African Development Bank, 2009, Pemunta and Mbu-Arrey, 2013). The country's land tenure legislation has evolved from communal land ownership among clan members to single ownership by the colonial masters but coexists with "customary" or "traditional" land tenure. The Germans introduced registration in the *Grunduch* (German land register) as the principle of land securitization which largely favoured German colonialists who occupied vast swathes of fertile land in the coastal areas of Southwest Cameroon for plantation agriculture (Pemunta and Fonmboh, 2010). There has also been significant shifts from traditional and intermediate forms of land occupation including purchase, and the lease of land among others for commercial purposes under the combined effect of the imbrication of rural communities into the market economy through the "commodity and value chain" (Ciccantell and Smith, 2009:361).

Following the unification of British and French Cameroon in 1972, a land reform was introduced in 1974 harmonizing the legal land systems used in the country. Since then, Ordinance No. 74/1 and 74/2 of 6 July 1974 establishing the rules governing land tenure and State lands respectively and laws and decrees amending and implementing them, as well as Law No.85/09 of 4 July 1985 relating to expropriation for public purposes and conditions of compensation constitute the regulatory framework for cadastral survey and land management in Cameroon.

The 1974 Lands Ordinance stipulates that all farmers who have peacefully occupied and productively appropriated a given piece of land prior to 1974 may step forward to register and receive legal title to that land. While the ordinance provided rural farmers with concrete boundary markers, rather than formal titles, these markers grant neither legal rights nor protection. Furthermore, they do not give access to credit markets. A conjuncture between high cost and time (6.3 years on the average), bureaucracy and corruption has stymied the attempt of poor farmers to avail themselves of the Ordinance and to obtain land titles. In the wake of the SAP, the government of Cameroon slashed funding for the Lands Department and increased the titling fee. This implied additional official and unofficial financial burden for land title applicants. The overall consequence is that:

> Farmers initiate the title process and pay the fees necessary to have state agents place concrete boundary markers on their land. They then abandon

their application and pay no additional fees (Firmin-Sellers and Sellers, 1999:1120).

Land titles which are another form of territorialization have remained the preserve of men: mostly politicians, bureaucrats and businessmen. Boundary markers are only symbolic of an individual's occupation of the land. The Ordinance further prohibits the titling of under or undeveloped land. This has given the lee-way for administrators to engage in the selective registration of undeveloped land. According to the letter and spirit of the Ordinance, the state will award titles only to the individual who has invested in the land, and only when that investment is sufficiently large. While the concept of sufficient investment is relative, it has a resonance with the colonial land tenure regime of "effective occupation as development." (Pemunta 2013) Additionally, the Ordinance is antithetical to the widespread custom that obliges family and lineage heads to hold land in trust, and to redistribute parcels of land to future generations of family members (Firmin-Sellers and Sellers, 1999:1117-18). The colonial and postcolonial state's usurpation of societal authority heralded the signature tune of capitalism through the control of land as a significant factor of production. This replication of the colonial state's claim over land and natural resources is eloquently captured by Njoh's observation that present-day postcolonial land laws (the 1974 Cameroon Land Ordinance and its constellation of ordinances and amendments enacted thereafter) are 'ironically bolder and less tolerant of customary entitlements and rights to land.' It came to replace the traditional land regime with one rooted in the capitalist value system (Njoh 1992b:25 citing Njoh, 1988:411-2).

A World Bank report intimates that 'more than 50% of Cameroonians with registered land at the surveys office are public employees and only 5% are farmers'(cf. African Development Bank, 2009:2). A conjuncture between bureaucracy, high cost and lack of social capital has excluded smallholder farmers from the land registration process (Pemunta, 2013:12). It has concurrently given politicians, "bureaucrats, highly ranked civil servants, and traders" leverage, while "male, let alone female, farmers" (Van den Berg, 1997:192, see also, Noorduyn, 2005:80) are eased out of the process. Both state and corporate dispossession which has turned members of local communities into "virtual land owners and tenants" (Pemunta, 2013) is embedded in the colonial era concept of "undeveloped" land as well as the primacy of written law over customary law and rights. This notion of "effective occupation as development" has wright violence on local communities. In the colonial era, effective occupation meant that land had to be used for large-scale agriculture, without which it was considered as "empty," "unoccupied" and therefore as "no man's land." During German colonial rule in Cameroon, and as a ruse to justify the expropriation of land for large-scale plantation projects, "land ownership entailed registration in the German land register-*Grunbuch*, without which it was attributed the status of State or "Crown land." This practice became institutionalized during the Franco-British colonial rule preceding World War 1. This ensured the uninterrupted control and supply of natural resources to the metropolis at the detriment of local inhabitants, most of whom were smallholder farmers (Norduyn, 2005:78, Pemunta, 2013:10). Export-oriented commercial agriculture was prioritized at the expense of subsistence farming. This Eurocentric framework and colonial script of "private property" has been copied and replicated and has become the mantra of postcolonial African state's land tenure legislation and spatial practices leading to the dispossession of local communities. Operationalized through the creation of protected areas and plantations, this colonial developmentalism policy tied and continues to link the Global South to the economic apron of the developed world. 'Developmental Eurocentrism' (Dussel, 1999, Amin, 1980, Escobar, 1995) reproduced its forces "by continuing the pattern of resource expropriation and economic control by the industrialized country" (Pemunta and Fonmboh, 2010:40), which has led to the pattern of economic dependency and in the perpetuation of underdevelopment in most of the Third World (Amin, 1980, Escobar, 1995). Like in the colonial era, countries of the global South are under huge "pressure from powerful international agencies to raise exports and open markets, implying importing natural resources/commodities at low prices and manufactured goods at high prices" (Pemunta and Fonmboh, 2010:40). Apart from the re-enactment of the colonial Eurocentric and econocentric model of 'development' which was embedded in the separation of economic from social development: "once wealth was[is] created, nation states could address the social aspects of development" (Ibid), the phenomenon of land grabs (which some optimists present as a "win-win" situation) further encapsulates deep transformations in the meaning of land and private property. The imposition of this Western capitalist worldview is leading to myriad problems: displacement of rural populations, unemployment, urbanization and environmental destruction (Baneerjee and Linstead, 2001, cf. Pemunta and Fonmboh, 2010:40). Colonialism was underpinned by the profit motive of exploiting raw materials and labour and not the desire for the socioeconomic development of the various regions and ethnic homelands of the colonies.

> Therefore, regions that were neither significant centres of colonial economic production, nor situated along the major centres of the colonial system of communication and administration suffered socio-economically (Nnoli, 1980:28).

Similarly, Tatah Mentan notes that colonialism was largely a profit-making venture through the "underdevelopment of colonies in the interests of the imperialists" (Mentan, 20011:19). This has eventuated in victims (labourers), who are subordinated to the colonial state and beneficiaries (capitalists) with local and global linkages. The colonial state became the mechanism for surplus appropriation and redistribution. In the postcolonial context, the state '[is] the dominant economic agent and channel of accumulation, and ...state accumulation [is] intimately entangled with individual mobility, power and wealth' (Bayart, 1986, Gledhill, 2000:101-102, Pemunta and Fonmboh, 2010:40). The cumulative outcome of this appropriation with its attendant state-level redistribution has 'engendered corruption [and] the result [is] a distorted and unproductive capitalism (underdevelopment) where wealth [is] completely dissociated from entrepreneurial activity.' This has subsequently given rise to confusion, multi-level conflict, inequalities, class crystallization, among others (Mentan, 20011:19). It is therefore unsurprising that the Ndian and kupemanenguba Divisions- the sites of the Herakles plantation owes their few dilapidated infrastructure only to the establishment of Pamol Plantation Plc for the extraction of palm nuts and palm oil since mineral resources are carted away through the sea.

Compounding the state's monopoly over land and natural resources and engendering further exclusion and violence is the fact that "the corporate nature of customary land rights" is legally unenforceable under the 1974 land reform for "... any sale or alienation of unregistered land by the customary community is illegal" (Fisiy, 1992:52). This situation bears resonances to Annelies Zoomers's observation that "land rights are always more complex than public versus private" (Zoomers, 2001:14). According to Cameroon's 1974 land Ordinance, and its subsequent decrees and modifications, there are three categories of land- two regimes of registered land-private or public as well as non-registered "common pool" [national land]. This legislation is not in tune with local level circumstances (values, customs or interests) and has given the state undue leverage by making it the de jure owner of all land and natural resources (Pemunta, 2013:13). This has led to a situation where indigenous elites, bureaucrats, and cattle grazers are increasingly using their positions of authority and wealth to amass large tracts of land for the establishment of cattle ranches and plantations, mostly at the detriment of the rural masses whose livelihood depends on land (Munge, 2012:89).

Within the context of neoliberalism, the state controls people and their relations to natural resources including land through the mechanism of the of "the production of territory" (Vandergeest and Peluso, 1995:387, Brenner and Elden, 2009, see also Brenner, 2001). The supremacy of legal over customary land tenure regimes permits the neoliberal Cameroon state to act as an agent for the commodification of its territory, thereby acquiring 'an unprecedented supremacy over other regulatory operations within the state's institutional architecture' (Brenner, 2001:799). Physical space as territory is a historically and geographically located site, stake and outcome of power relations and political thought (Vandergeest and Peluso, 1995:355), as well as a space of inclusion and exclusion.

'Exclusion' from 'State Space'?

The Southwest Region where the Herakles Farms plantation is being established has long had a coastal plantation economy as an outcome of German colonial rule (1884-1914). The setting up of oil palm plantation is one way of producing territory and simultaneously entails the production of local and international spaces. The production of oil palm, bananas and rubber linked the area to the national and the international capitalist system. The area has however continued to be marginalized and dispossessed. The colonial plantation attracted huge numbers of migrant workers largely from other parts of Cameroon but also from Nigeria into the region. When Cameroon became an enemy property following the German defeat in World War 1, the plantations were reverted to the British colonial administration in tandem with the recommendations of the League of Nations. Ndian Division is host to one of the two agro-industrial complexes that have held sway in the Western plantation sector in Cameroon: Pamol. Initially owned by Unilever, it was put in the market through a public-private partnership in October 1987. The Division also hosts parts of the parastatal, the Cameroon Development Corporation (CDC). Ndian borders Eastern Nigeria and is the location of the Rio Del Rey and the once contested rich oil and fish Bakassi peninsula between Nigeria and Cameroon. It can be aptly described as

> one of the most important areas in the country: it possesses large oil palms [and mineral resources]. Paradoxically, despite its natural riches, it continues to be one of the most isolated and marginalized regions in the country (Konings, 2011:509).

This suggests Ndian's simultaneous 'exclusion' from 'state space' (Brenner and Elden, 2001:362), and 'state failure' despite its enormous natural resources as well as the urgent need to transform it into a developmentalizable entity. Ndian is simultaneously an area where state spaces are contested. Conceptions of territory and power are highly complex, and political space is conceived as a multilayered structure of concentric circles of diminishing control, radiating from the various cores (Kopytoff, 1987:29, see also Bennafla, 2013).

The unpaved road network constructed in the seventies has deteriorated because of lack of maintenance, remains seasonal and impassable in the rainy season. This trans-border region is far more integrated into the Nigerian economy-influx of Nigerian fishermen, traders and peasants, legal and illegal trade-than to the Cameroonian economy. Most of the fish mongers (90%) are of Nigerian nationality principally from the Ibiobio and Ijaw ethnicities of the Akwa-Ibom and Cross River states respectively. Furthermore, the marine artisanal fishing industry in the Division is largely dependent on, and interwoven with the Nigeria economy (Kamphorst, 1994:v). It has been recognized that trans-border communities in borderlands are characterized by different, co-existing and simultaneous identities giving rise to confusion about one's identity-showing the very dynamism of the concept of identity in borderlands (Pemunta and Aristide, 2013:280) where in complicity with state agents, economic subversion takes place (Bennafla, 20133:231).

Political reasons have been invoked to account for Ndian Division's historic marginalization and neglect. It has been characterized as a "no man's land" because of its peripheral location and therefore away from the "enclave economy." During the interwar years the British showed no interest in its development. Initially part of Kumba Division, it became a full-fleshed administrative Division in 1967, but no funds were allocated for its development by the state of Cameroon. It is alleged that this neglect was politically motivated for 95% of its population allegedly voted in the 1961 plebiscite in favour of integration with Nigeria rather than for reunification with French speaking Cameroon. Nerius Mbile, one of its legendary political leaders is on record for having allegedly declared that they were "irrevocably [bent] never to accept union with the Cameroon Republic.' 'If on this we shall have to be killed to the last man' he pledged, 'it should rather be better that history records how a race of men died to the men fighting over their freedom' (John, 1970:166, cf Konings, 2011:510).

The neoliberal state facilitates the production and reproduction of territory using diverse strategies-both institutional and extra-institutional, across myriad geographical sites and scales (Brenner and Elden, 2009:369). These strategies, largely technocratic, but also apolitical operate in relation to the question of mondialisation (globalisation) (Brenner and Elden, 2009:318)-subscription to the neoliberal global project and agenda. Among these strategies are territorial cohesion and integration, mechanisms for addressing territorial inequalities, and state developmental strategies to promote certain spaces as sites for capitalist accumulation (Ibid:369). This triple strategy encompasses territorial configurations in the form of large plantations, protected areas and national parks, special economic zones (SEZ) and transportation infrastructure to sustain economic activities (see also Vandergeest and Peluso, 1995:387). Secondly, the spatial practice of "taming" territories (Massey, 2005) is operationalized through consent and coercion, practice and representation. First, the "taming" of territories involves the discursive practice of representations of imagined developments, identities and geographies "designed to shape and reshape" territorial spaces into nationalized, nationalizing unities within a broader framework defined by the "world market" (Brenner and Elden, 2009:369). Secondly, they are embedded in policies and legal frameworks that facilitate the delineation and enforcement of projects. Thirdly, they necessitate the use of force, violence and fear-arrests and imprisonment of opposition voices. The State-Herakles concession agreement explicitly mandates Herakles Farms to arrest and imprison anyone "trespassing" on its land concession. This is a mechanism of ruling and shaping the territorial spaces occupied by the oil palm entrepreneur so as to ensure a conducive business climate. Without outrightly discounting studies based on the Dutch disease (Ross, 2004, Collier and Hoeffer, 2004, Collier, 2004) arguments that link the causal explanations for violence to extractable resources, we subscribe to the political ecology perspective of violence and war as facilitating the construction of territory as a state space (Peluso and Vandergeest, 2011). Lastly, as a coercive tool, fear paralyzes and discipline individual and collective actions and imaginations, thereby giving more leverage for control and domination (Martinez, 2011:25-26).

The Herakles Farms plantation is sandwiched between the Ndian (30,600ha) and KupeMuanengouba (42,600ha) Divisions of Southwest Cameroon. The concession lies in an area where the protection of nature and conservation through the creation of the contiguous Korup National Park (KNP) and other protected areas has already led to the ceding of enormous parcels of land for these development and conservation projects as well as for the resettlement of 'conservation refugees.' These conservation-driven acts of enclosure are forms of violence, even when they are void of the use of force because '…states have rarely provided equivalent livelihood alternatives or adequate compensation for evictees' (Neumann, 2001:308). They are separated from their means of production. Other forms of violence visited on people who are resettled due to exclusionary conservation include: increased risks of landlessness, joblessness, loss of subsistence, marginalization, homelessness, food insecurity, loss of access to common property, death and social disarticulation (Schmidt-Soltau 2003). Exclusionary conservation has resonances with the colonial perception of Africans as misusing nature, as unable to manage the human-nature relationship, self-govern themselves as well as the criminalization of their previous normal daily activities (Dunn, 2009:436, Brockington, 2002).

Neoliberalism, Conservation and Territorialization

Neoliberalism involves the integration of the economy with environmental protection measures that are sustained by international, regional and sub-regional treaties and conventions dealing with natural resource management as well as civil society provisioning of state services. It further involves the simultaneous conservation of the environment and the promotion of economic growth (Castree 2008:142, Corson 2011:705, World Commission on Environment and Development (WCED), 1987). The crafting of Cameroon's new environmental legislation, the 1994 Forestry Law was driven by global forces- particularly the World Bank and conservation NGOs through 'public-private partnerships.' Although state territorialisation under neoliberalism was driven, developed and managed by a network of alliances comprised of state, private and not-for-profit (transnational entities), it was not a state-led process. By negotiating protected area boundaries, these actors determined acceptable rights and uses, claims to forest lands, the authority to craft forest policy and the authority to determine who could accumulate from these forests (Corson, 2011:703, see also Vandergeest and Peluso, 1995:385). In Cameroon, this territorialisation process coincided with a severe economic crisis during which park management budgets plummeted, leading to the degradation of infrastructure and logistical services. The SAP led to the downsizing of the public service payroll and a 50% reduction in salary. The end result included corruption, desertion and neglect of responsibilities in the public service (Bauer, 2003:23). The SAP also led to a mismatch between population growth and the provision of social amenities. This resulted in natural resource degradation in rural areas where there is overdependence on the exploitation of natural resources-fuel wood, building materials, wildlife game, parkland, herbs, medicinal plants and habitat for other ecosystems and wildlife (Fonjong 2006). It has been well established that internationally propelled national forestry processes tend to encounter massive implementation challenges (Smouts, 2001) including lack of autonomy, ownership and inclusiveness. They are acts of global governmentality regimes upon regions, their people and their natural resources. Protected areas, be they national parks are 'contested state spaces': places where officially sanctioned state-making practices are successfully challenged, resisted and replaced by alternatives" (Dunn, 2009:423). They tend to create conflicts between protected areas, erase traditional usage rights as communities are excluded from decision-making and planning. Furthermore, conservation has been dogged by an external impetus to deforestation in the form of logging by foreign and multinational companies. While foreign logging concessions and parliament were against reforms, there was the lack of "an implementation strategy that is compatible with the underlying dynamics of political and socio-economic changes in Cameroon" by key stakeholders such as the World Bank (Essama-Nssah and Gockwoski, 2000). Additionally, contrary to the spirit of the 1994 Forestry Law and the 1996 Constitution as well as associated decrees of application, there is no channeling of proceeds accruing from the exploitation of natural resources for development in the production areas. This has led to accusations of 'internal colonialism' by locals and Anglophone separatist movements including the Southern Cameroon National Council (SCNC) (see Nkwi and Nyamjoh, 2011). This resonates with what Vandergeest and Peluso (1995:385) describe as 'internal territorialization'- that is territoriality as a socially and geographically rooted, but contested process through which a state institution 'establishes control over natural resources and the people who use them' within national boundaries. As Peluso (2005:13) maintains territorialization is '[a] dynamic and contingent process, an expression of relationships that emerge, operate, and converge across and within localities, national spaces and global networks.'

Emboldened by the recommendations of the Rio Earth Summit and the Fifth World Parks Congress (Durban, South Africa), the government of Cameroon decided to increase the number of existing protected areas and national parks. These global policy frameworks were subsequently translated through the establishment and gazzetment of national parks and protected areas (Pas) void of any human activities. As of 2005, 14% of Cameroon's territory had been earmarked as PAs. In 2012, Cameroon counted 25 national parks. From 2006-2011 the portion of land allocated to PAs increased by 8% to 7.4 million hectares (16%) of total national land area and 43% of the total National Forestry Estate (NFE). This was the outcome of the creation of 10 new national parks, many of which resulted from the reclassification of forest reserves (Mertens et al., 2012:29). As pristine wilderness reserves, NPs are isolated from adverse human impacts, but are simultaneously made available to the public (Lowry 1994) for education and tourism, development and media contracts. The creation/expansion of these protected areas involved three components of territorialization-'mapping boundaries, establishing and enforcing new rights, and determining acceptable resource uses'(Corson 2011:705) under the auspices of conservation NGOs such as the Worldwide Fund for Nature, IUCN and foreign aid donors including the World Bank and the IMF.

The KNP was one of several internationally funded conservation initiatives "set up to assist African governments to manage protected areas" (Malleson 2000:24) by linking conservation and development through the Integrated Conservation and Development (ICDPs) projects paradigm. The main partner implementing the ICDP project was the Worldwide Fund for Nature. Although an improvement to "fines and fences" approaches to conservation in protected areas involving the devolution of power, as well as the involvement of forest dwellers as conservation stakeholders, Community-based Natural Resource Management (CBNRM) continues to be a form of fortress conservation as well as a form of territorialization. The underlying ideology has remained the prioritization of forest and animals at the expense of the local population. It is a reflection of the "colonial-people-exclusion-strategy" (Fonjong, 2006:670) aimed at pulling resource users into new market economies while relieving local people of their land and/or resources and obliging them to become dependent on an industry (often ecotourism) over which they have no leverage and from which they earn very little money (Kelly 2011:686). The adoption of co-management meaning the devolution of responsibilities implied a reduction in workload. It further implied that the high investment cost of conservation could be shouldered by international donors who were eager to finance fashionable international conservation and development programmes (Bauer, 2003:23-24). The protection of natural resources through enclosures which underpins the international conservation agenda is actually about the protection of resources for purposes of capital accumulation by a host of actors (Corson 2011:707). It is also about making claims by non-state actors. As Sikor and Lund (2009) acknowledge, state as well as non-state actors claim the attribute of governance through territorialization. The creation of protected areas is a form of primitive accumulation that involves both enclosure and the dispossession of land and natural resources through the dissolution of the commons and accumulation (Kelly 2011:683).

The Herakles concession site lies inside the world recognized KNP (125,000ha) biodiversity hotspot and between other globally significant protected areas-key habitats for primates, elephants, buffaloes and a wide range of scarce, endemic and the International Union for Conservation of Nature (IUCN) Red-listed species of animals. Plant species reported in the park include 480 species of herbs. The park has a unique record of more than 400 species of birds, 82 reptiles, 92 amphibians, and about 1000 species of butterflies. Aquafauna consists of 130 different fish species and there are over 160 mammal species[1]. The creation of the Rumpi Forest Reserve took up 45,675 hectares, Ndongore Park, 230,000 hectares, Palmol Plantation Limited 11,000 hectares, culminating in a total of 448,885 hectares of existing land[2]. There is therefore an important threat to both national and international conservation due to direct damage to flora and wildlife habitats as a result of conversion to oil palm plantation. Additionally, these protected areas are suffering from ineffective surveillance and policing mechanisms along their boundaries, especially along the KNP boundaries. Worse still, the government has granted logging concessions to international logging companies in areas bordering these protected areas. Allegations are rife that these companies are removing species other than those they have declared. Observations at various sites of the Herakles concession showed that Herakles was involved in illegal logging. Hunting and the trapping of bush meat using high caliber weapons as well as the collection and processing of NTFPs are the life wire of the local economy. Locals constantly undertake illegal timber exploitation for the production of planks. They also use gammalin to catch fish. These protected

---

1 Korup National Park - The Displacement of the Indigenous People: Voluntary or by Force?. University for Peace and Conflict. Retrieved 21 February 2013.

2 https://www.savewildlife.com/downloads/save_the_forest/Ngolo_chiefs_letter_of_opposition_to_SGSOC.pdf.

areas are under serious threats due to collusion between park guards and illegal poachers from and outside of the community (Mbile et al., 2005, cf. Pemunta and Mbu-Arrey, 2013:20) as well as petty corruption among guards leading to loss of incentive to police the forest and to report illegal logging to forest protection agencies. Locals constantly complain that Herakles Farms is already involved in illegal logging and since they own the resources, it is better they exploit it as much as possible before Herakles grabs everything from them.

> Is there any need for conservation when Herakles is engaged in the blatant and illegal harvesting of our timber in the same area we are told to conserve, and from which we were driven away in the name of conservation? We have to make use of the resources here before it is too late. We are now acting like thieves in our own ancestral land. (Ebongo, Interview, 23 March, 2012).

Accentuating these challenges is the plummeting of park management budget, leading to degradation of infrastructure and logistical services (Pemunta and Mbu-Arrey, Ibid). This shortfall that began in the 1990s has had a negative effective on the conservation of protected areas all over Cameroon. Rumours are even making the rounds about the likelihood of the sale of the permanent forest by the state sale (Hoyle and Levang, 2012:9). There are heightened fears from past experiences that contrary to the Herakles plantation which is being paraded as a blessing because it will allegedly spike socio-economic development, like the activities and operations of the already existing Pamol plantations, it will become another "White Elephant" (Ibid).

> For decades, the government has in the name of development imposed hardship on us. What politicians are parading as development is far from that. Pamol spray their palms and we in heal the chemicals, we have no roads, no portable water. Herakles has only come to worsen our situation. They have taken our land and will soon send us to the wilderness (Ekongolo, Interview of 20th July 2010).

In terms of development, the area is backward. It is enclaved and has the most dangerous stretches of unpaved roads. Travelling within the administrative area is mostly through water. There is an acute shortfall of social amenities and personnel. It is paradoxically rich in mineral resources, evergreen forest and water courses. It harbours the rich oil and fish Bakassi peninsula and the world class Korup biodiversity reserve. Compounding the situation was the decade long Bakassi crisis pitting Cameroon and Nigeria over the ownership of the Bakassi peninsula (surface area of 665 square km) and its natural resources. Even after the official ceding of the peninsula to Cameroon through the Green Tree Agreement, insecurity still reigns in the area. Pirates and militant groups from the Niger Delta constantly kidnap and ransom the inhabitants. Heightening during the crisis, and presently, the inhabitants are still suffering from constant, untold hardship from various groups of pirates and the Nigerian and Cameroonian military. They are subjected to harassment; brutality, extortion, destruction of the economy, the sacking and destruction of villages, broken family and community life, environmental pollution and stench from unburied corpses (see also recorderline.blogspot.hu). As Janet Roitman (2004) notes contemporary economic practices and networks are characterized by smuggling, banditry and extortion. Although these activities are not a questioning of regulatory authority per se, they are a resurgence of the brutal logics of regulation embedded in Central African society where military-commercial networks of illegal but socially legitimated economic activity challenge the authority of the state while perpetuating its grip on power (see also Roitman, 2007). The area has historically suffered from decades of deprivation, oppression and pauperization. This is reminiscent of 'internal colonialism' from both the colonial masters and from the Francophone-dominated postcolonial Cameroonian state (see Vandergeest and Peluso, 1995:385). Trans-border spaces are 'peripheral spaces, away from political and administrative centres' where [economic and political] underdevelopment is usually a lived reality' (Pemunta and Aristide, 2013:280,284). Such areas are often characterized by the co-existence of regulated and unregulated economic activities that have transformed international border spaces into hubs of lucrative business and economic mobility. Unregulated economic activities undertaken in borderland areas include networks of actors trading in black market petrol, small arms, drugs, and stolen 4-wheel drive vehicles among others (Roitman, 2007:189, see also Bennafla, 2013). The Rio Del Rey Basin, the source of 75% of Cameroon's crude oil exports which peaked production to 158,000 barrels per day in the late 1970s, but petered out in the mid-1980s is found in Ndian Division. Paradoxically, the area is however bereft of hospitals, paved roads, schools, telephone facilities, as well as fuel stations. A household story in Cameroon has it that when Honourable Nwalipenja Lobe Ekwele did muster the courage and bravery to ask former Cameroon President Amadou Ahidjo about oil money and why his Division of origin (Ndian) had oil but lacked basic infrastructure, the latter did not only keep him waiting for endless hours, he addressed him thus in pidgin English:

> Nwanlipepe (a deformation of his name), you de ask moni for oya, na you mami é oya?" Nwalipepe you de ask money for oyan, na you papa é oyan? Oyan weh de for sea na for all people, make I know hear you talk about oya again[3].

My translation:

> Nwalipenja, you are asking about oil money, is it your mother's oil, is it your father's oil? Oil that is in the sea is for everyone. Let me not hear you talk about oil again.

This implies that mineral wealth is seen as a national asset. This is the case since the state lays claim to all parcels of land and the mineral resources therein. According to this reasoning those on whose land these resources are found are not entitled to any special privileges. This resonates with Lazare Essimi Menye, former finance minister's declaration downplaying the importance of Ndian to Cameroon's economy by comparing the availability of oil in Ndian to cocoa production from his native Lekie Division in the Centre Region. He barefacedly maintained that the availability of oil wealth in Ndian does not entitle the people to development projects. This seems to suggest that the elites are rather entitled to political opportunities within bureaucratic state structures. After all, with the centralization of power over natural resource wealth, especially oil, the revenue allocation principle of derivation that proposes revenue allocation proportionate to contribution to national revenue has never been applied to Anglophone Cameroon in general and Ndian Division in particular. This situation has fueled sentiments of secession among Anglophone nationalists of all hues and colours as they constantly invoke the pathetic tragedy of the 'resource minorities of Ndian.'(see also Nkwi and Nyamnjoh 2011). In line with its policy of divide and rule, Nwalipenja was later "co-opted into the hegemonic alliance of private gains" (Mentan, 2011:19) as Minister Plenipotentiary and simultaneously Board Member of the National Investment Corporation, until his death in 2005 as a strategy to lull him to sleep. Frances Stewart usefully notes that political, cultural, and economic factors are instrumental in constructing group identities by political leaders who appropriate group cohesion by mobilizing it as a powerful mechanism in their competition for power and resources by adopting a strategy of the "reworking of historical memories to engender group identity" (Steward, 2000:246-7).

[3] http://www.orokousa.org/orokoland/economy.html.

Whereas the state-Herakles alliance parade the Herakles Farm plantation as an act of charity and philanthropy meant to bring "development, growth and employment," it should rather be seen as a "taming" (Massey, 2005) strategy meant to ensure market-led economic development through (1) a benevolent integration of this peripheral region into the centre, a mechanism for addressing the historical territorial inequality and exclusion. Furthermore, it is also a state developmental strategy to promote Ndian Division as a new frontier of capital accumulation given its oil wealth. Despite its largely undelivered social welfare components, the aim of the Herakles project is to facilitate the extractive economy for the "national common good." That is a means of connecting the region into the government's agenda as a potential 'developmentalizable entity' (Escobar, 2008:161). Antonio Gramsci's concept of hegemony is appropriate here. By hegemony, we understand that most members of society reach a consensus in which their needs, behaviours and expectations coalesce with the needs of "the productive forces for development, and hence, [correspond] with the interest of the ruling class. To achieve this form of political power, the state builds an ideological and intellectual discourse capable of winning the consent and endorsement of its citizens. Therefore, a Neoliberal historic bloc becomes hegemonic when it succeeds in allying its interest, with that of the rest of society, and therefore achieves unanimity of not only economic and political aims, but also, ideological and moral ones (Gramsci, 1971:258).

The inhabitants of the Ndian and Kupemuanengouba Divisions of the Southwest Region like 80% of Cameroon's rural population are involved in subsistence agriculture. These smallholder farmers cultivate crops such as cassava, palm oil, and bananas. Excesses are sold on the local market to meet household needs. They also produce cash crops like cocoa-a male crop characterized by a gendered division of labour in the production cycle. While women are mainly involved in foodstuff production, they also assist their husbands in the cocoa farms. The area is saturated with oil palms in the wilderness: "Palm oil is to us like water is to the sea. We do not need another oil palm factory here" (Amin, Interview, 20 March, 2012). Palm oil is processed on an artisanal basis to supply unrefined (red) oil for local consumption and sale. Women are involved in the gathering of forest products such as bush mangoes (*Irvingia gabonesis*), monkey cola (*cola lepidota*) and bush pepper. Greenpeace International (2013a) concedes that women derive an estimated 30% of their cash incomes from forest products. Plantation jobs are more likely to lead to deeper poverty for local farmers. It has been estimated that an average cocoa farmer in the area presently earns almost twice per annum as an agricultural labourer at Pamol-the nearby industrial oil palm producer in Ndian Division. This is happening against the heightened backdrop of tenure insecurity which is gendered and more accentuated among women, as well as exploitation by cocoa traders (see also Greenpeace, 2013a).

NEOLIBERALISAM, PRIVATISATION AND TERRITORIALIZATION

Under tremendous pressure from international multilateral institutions spearheaded by the World Bank and the IMF, Cameroon grudgingly adopted neoliberal privatization as a macro-economic policy to jump start its moribund economy. In the agricultural sector, neoliberal reforms were however adopted without any meaningful land reforms which are the very pivot of socio-economic development. As Corson (2011) rightly observes, state territorialization under neoliberalism, including the creation or expansion of national parks was driven by both state and non-state actors and is not a state-controlled process. Although David Harvey (2003:154) argues that the incentives for state power to back capitalist investments can either be internally or externally driven by multilateral institutions like the World Bank and the IMF, he however tacitly acknowledges that the process often requires a combination of both for: 'keeping the territorial and capitalistic logics of power intertwined…'(Ibid, 2003:145). By aiming for integration into the circuit of global capitalism, the state provides a "facilitative regime and adequate opportunities" for capital through mechanisms such as privatization, low corporate tax regimes or a conducive business environment" (Harvey, 2006:xxv). For instance, Herakles' contract with the State of Cameroon stipulated that the company pays an annual rent of US$1(500FCFA) for the lease of the land per ha for land in use and 0.5 US$ (250FCFA) per ha for undeveloped land. Secondly, since the continuity of capital flow "rests upon the existence of adequate institutional arrangements that facilitate the continuity of that flow across space and time," creating and sustaining these arrangements becomes a leading preoccupation of the hegemonic state (Harvey, 2010:69, see also Harvey, 2003). However, the implementation of attempts to "roll back" the state in Cameroon has been dogged by corrupt practices and cronyism leading to the ceding away of public enterprises at give away prices. In his assessment of the privatization process in Sub-Saharan Africa, Thiery A. Buch rightly notes that "privatization has created new political patronage opportunities, leading to numerous corruption scandals which have damaged the credibility of the privatization process" (Buchs, 2003:1, see also Van De Walle, 1989:609). This has resonances with the view that "...traditional Cameroon social policies are widely known for their clientelism, corruption, and failure to reach the poorest" (Mentan, 2011:36). This suggests that policies that subject the majority to market forces, in the name of 'market civilisation' (Hale, 2005:12) tend to preserve "social protection for the strong" (Gill, 2003:119). They are the concretization of a neoliberal discourse. Cameroon has further, (in)advertently favoured large-scale export-oriented agribusiness by ceding large portions of land through the process of "accumulation by dispossession" (Harvey, 2005) to foreign interests who apart from floating national and international environmental standards, export most of their produce at the detriment of the local economy in the name of "development," "poverty alleviation" and "growth." The establishment convention between the GoC and Herakles does not include clauses obliging Herakles to sell its products on the local market. The company plans to export a portion of its projected 400,000 metric tons (MT) of crude palm oil and 40,000 MT of palm kernel oil per year, while leaving some for domestic consumption in Cameroon "depending on market conditions" (Social and Environmental Impact Assessment (ESIA). Furthermore, Herakles Farms's contract requires it to hire 80% Cameroonian labour only after five years into the project. However, failure to comply with the 80% threshold target, must simply be explained and there is no penalty for noncompliance. Thus, uncertainty looms over how many Cameroonians will actually be employed by the project and for how long their employment contracts will last. Additionally, it is murky whether Cameroon's minimum wage laws and other labour protection measures apply to employees since the contract allows for the company to pay employees according to "minimum wage scales fixed on the basis of productivity and efficiency criteria" and to freely negotiate terms of employee dismissal (Ibid)[4].

While private and public investments in agriculture is required "policies that transfer land to investors motivated principally by a concern to feed populations in other countries, supply biofuel markets across the globe, especially the EU and US, or to secure speculative profit" (Africa Progress Report 2012,cf. Geary, 2012:7) have been deplored by transnational civil society actors. This does not however presuppose a victimary view of the state.

[4] Establishment Convention By and Between the Republic of Cameroon and SG Sustainable Oils Cameroon PLC.Section 9.6 (a, b, c).http://Cameroon veritas. files.wordpress.com/ 2011/08/ sgsoc-convention1.pdf.

The instrumentalist view presents the state as a tool/victim open to manipulation by transnational corporations and foreign governments. Although Henri LeFebvre recognizes the high stakes and therefore higher quantity of power of multinationals in "negotiation" processes, he however maintains that nation-states do not always have to give in to subordination, but "[should rather] resist imperialisms and [should, and can] negotiate with global firms" (Lefebvre 1979 [2001:778]. One way of conducting this negotiation is that both national and international standard business practices, social and environmental procedures are followed to the letter. Following Lefebvre, a strong and vibrant civil society that provides oversight can restrain the state from selling itself as well as the country in the world market (Ibid.:778) through processes such as privatization including land grabs that are often shrouded in illegality and confidentiality. Land grabs which is a form of territorialization as well as 'internal colonialism,' the World Bank notes; take place mostly in countries known for their lax laws and corruption (World Bank, 2011:15). Most often, international investors and companies are not transparent in their dealings with African governments (Obi, 2009:113-114).

Apart from extremely generous investment terms-particularly generous tax breaks- including a total exemption from all taxes and duties for ten years, the annual 'area rent' to be paid by Herakles Farms was estimated at US66,000 annually as per the 2009 Convention Agreement, "once all of the land is planted" is quite minimal. The nitty-gritty of the "revised convention" endorsed by the presidential decree of November 25, 2013 granting a temporary concession remains opaque. The decree cedes 19,843 hectares for three years renewable depending on their ability to respect engagements. This is happening after Herakles Farms has been operating in illegality for four years. Contrary to the 99 years at FCFA 500 per hectare, the company is now expected to pay FCFA 3300 per hectare per year (259 billion FCFA per annum) to the state alongside a land tax of FCFA 198,430,000 million for the same period. Even more disturbing, in collusion with GoC, Herakles Farms has failed to make full disclosures for reasons of "confidentiality." This is contrary to several international standards including the requirements of the International Finance Corporation (IFC) (see International Finance Corporation, 2012). Herakles Farms' business activities are tainted with illegality. The company began its operations without any properly granted lease under Cameroon law.

National laws warrant that a land lease agreement of above 50 hectares can only be authorized by the president. Moreover, the development of nurseries has been without compliance with the minimum legal requirement of conducting a satisfactory environmental and social impact assessment. Furthermore, the company has been involved in indiscriminate planting of survey beacons purporting to demarcate areas of land without due authorization and in total disregard of existing farms, sacred sites and village settlements.

Lack of Prior, Informed Consent

Even without the prior, informed consent of communities that would be most affected by the establishment convention between the government of Cameroon and Herakles Farms ceding 73,083 hectares for the cultivation of oil palm is a violation of the human and community rights of the local communities. Furthermore, the company is still to secure widespread consent and instead faces stiff resistance from several village communities. Respondents maintained that the company held no public consultations and that their "go betweens" organized only informal meetings. These individuals included Hon. Chief Mbile erstwhile Member of Parliament of the ruling Cameroon People's Democratic Movement (CPDM) party who was initially opposed to the project, but within four weeks backtracked. He is today the Community Base Officer (CBO) of Herakles Farms. Apart from acting as agent, he allegedly assigns who goes around corrupting those vigorously opposed to the project. Like in the Niger Delta, the "pro-company group of local chiefs and elite faction is ambivalent or Janus-faced: one face for the people, the other... for its transnational partners" (Obi, 2009:123). Chief Tabi Napoleon of Baro-Upper Balong discounted claims by Herakles that the company undertook a participatory consultation process prior to starting its activities:

> We only heard a plantation was coming to our area, bringing employment opportunities for our children. But we are realizing that our forest-our main source of livelihood is gradually being destroyed, putting the future of our children in danger. This is quite deceptive and unfortunate because our children will be deprived of land in the future on which to invest in, and the entire Nguti community, we have been told (by NGOs activists) is at the risk of relocation to places where we might find difficulties. We will have to leave behind our graveyards and sacred shrines, which will be destroyed, cutting us off from our ancestors (Interview of May 30, 2012).

Displacement of Native Population

There is overwhelming recognition and unanimity that large-scale land deals can lead to multiple vulnerabilities-land dispossession and exclusion from mineral resources, as well as to deeply entrenched poverty of smallholders, pastoralists, indigenous peoples and other rural communities (Pemunta, 2013, see IFAD, 2011:87, World Bank, 2011). In Colombia, this "accumulation by forced displacement and dispossession" caused widespread displacement of peasant farmers, a significant number of whom were Afro-Colombians. It further led to protracted violent conflicts and human rights abuses (Martinez, 2011:14). This has resonances with Tania Li's "centering [of] labour in the land grab debate" perspective according to which large scale farms do not only dispossess significant numbers of rural people from the land but also result in low absorption of their labour, because it is a "surplus" to the requirements of capital accumulation (Li 2011: 286). This implies that whereas land and resources are useful, people are not – and dispossession becomes disentangled from any prospect of labour absorption.

Unlawful Demarcation of Farmlands

Apart from illegally demarcating farmlands, Herakles launched its activities beginning in 2010 in violation of national law which requires that a Presidential decree sanctions such a concession. Specifically, a 1976 Law governing the allocation of concessions on state land requires that a decree be signed by the president and published (in both the French and English languages) in the official Gazette for any concession above 50 hectares. Herakles further opened an estimated 300ha, far above the 60ha tolerated by the law in the absence of a presidential land lease decree. The company then proceeded and planted portion of the land and piles of timber are awaiting auction. The company has also opened a 50 metres wide road linking Talangaye and Sambaliba whereas they received authorization for 15 metres (Dupuy and Achankap, 2013). Concurrently, Herakles further proceeded to the creation of nurseries for oil palms, without authorization for forest conversion, even prior to being issued a "Certificate of Environmental Conformity" by the Ministry of Environment, Nature Protection and Sustainable Development. In tandem with national legislation, this is a prerequisite for the creation of nurseries.

Lack of a Prior Environmental and Social Impact Assessment (ESIA)

Cameroon law warrants that a satisfactorily carried out ESIA pursuant to the provisions of Law No. 96/12 of 5 August, 1996 relating to environmental management and its decree of application No. 2005/0577/PM of 23 February 2005 laying down modalities for carrying out environmental impact assessment is a prerequisite to any large-scale project. Herakles Farms's action contradicts criterion 5.2 and 7.3 of the Roundtable on Sustainable Palm Oil (RSPO) which state that:

> The status of rare, threatened or endangered species and high conservation value habitats, if any, that exist in plantation or that could be affected by plantation or mill management, shall be identified and their conservation taken into accounts in management plans and operations.
>
> The first step is to conduct a comprehensive and participatory independent social environmental impact assessment(s) and the assessment(s) must include identification of primary forests, HCVA, areas of peat soil, and local people's land[5].

The company only produced and made public its highly controversial ESIA after protests and a Mundemba High Court ruling in a suit filed by the NGO, Struggle to Economize Future Environment (SEFE)[6,7], had temporarily barred it from proceeding with its acts on lands dependent on a mandatory ESIA so as to gauge the impact of their activities on the natural and human environment of the areas, and clearly outline concrete mitigating measures. Herakles actions also violate several of the eight International Finance Corporation (IFC) performance standards including:

> Performance Standard 1: [which] establishes the importance of (i) integrated assessment to identify the environmental and social impacts, risks, and opportunities of projects, (ii) effective engagement through disclosure of project-related information and consultation with local communities on matters that directly affect them, and (iii) the client's management of environmental and social performance throughout the life of the project.

---

[5] See http://www.rspo.org/en/rspo_and_hcv.

[6] See http://www.freundeskreis-partnerschaft-uebersee.de/uploads/media/UrteilMun demba 270212.pdf.

[7] The doctrine of locus standi in the area of human rights has been abolished by the Fundamental Rights (Enforcement Procedure) Rules 2009 which came into force on December 1, 2009.

> Performance Standards 2 through 8 establish objectives and requirements to avoid, minimize, and where residual impacts remain, to compensate/offset for risks and impacts to workers, affected communities, and the environment (International Finance Corporation, 2012:1).

Additionally, even the ESIA was tainted with illegality. The Ministry of Environment and Nature Protection violated the provisions of Article 12(i) of Decree No.2005/0577/pm of 23/02/2005 which states that "notice of public hearing of an ESIA must be given to the public at least 30 days in advance in a press release." Herakles deliberately fixed public hearings in Mundemba and Nguti from September 3rd, 2011 from 10 a.m to 4p.m. Curiously enough and contrary to the law on the matter, copies of the ESIA documents were not provided to opinion leaders, elites and other stakeholders in advance. Further compounding the situation, the public hearings were scheduled in the rainy season when the unpaved road network in the region are impassable thereby making it impossible for stakeholders to be present at the hearings. Despite the abovementioned irregularities, the company obtained a Certificate of Environmental Conformity from the Ministry on September 18, 2011-barely a couple of days after the "public hearings." This irregularity was challenged by SEFE at the Supreme Court and the court is still to dispose of the matter. The HCV received an unfavourable review by the Resource Network Technical Panel Peer Review released in April 2012. Specifically, the HCVRN peer review report alongside other important environmental and social considerations found the following inadequacies (1) lack of consideration of the wider landscape; 2) lack of clear definition of the methodology utilized in the classification of habitat quality; 3) underrepresentation of the land-use history; 4) no clear description of the consultation process undertaken; 5)lack of information on data collection methods, and f) inadequate use of the precautionary approach (HCV Resource Network Technical Panel Peer Review, 2012:3-5, Greenpeace, 2013)[8]. Additionally, the ESIA neither locate the 5 sites designated as oil mills in the project area nor examine their impacts on the environment.

[8] See also http://www.hcvnetwork.org/news-and-events/2013_heraklesletter.

ILLEGAL FELLING OF TREES AND TIMBER EXPLOITATION

The illegal felling of trees was observable at various sites including the Talangaye site. This illegality has also been documented by Greenpeace (Greenpeace, 2013, see also Dupuy and Achankap, 2013). This is contrary to the declarations of the Minister of Nature Protection, a native of Kupemanenguba Division, Philip Ngole Ngwese:

> We have sufficiently cautioned SGSOC against the dangers of felling trees and so most of their operations are limited outside the forest reserve zones. We call on you to give them your support and collaboration to enable the smooth operation of their activities. We have taken the necessary measures to ensure the mapped-out forest reserves in the Nguti area... are substantially preserved (Ngalame, 2012 cf.Alertnet.org).

Herakles is felling timber and damaging natural resources on which local livelihood systems are based. An inventory of the nursery site in Sambaliba identified even more exploitable timber than the first block with 11000m3 inventoried on 225ha. Timber evacuated from Fabe nursery site was either used by the company or allowed to decompose. Serious evidence of illegal timber exploitation has also been uncovered close to Fabe village with tracks opened by a caterpillar (GPS reading: 495697, 559880) (Dupuy and Achankap, 2013). Further compounding the situation is the fact that inexperienced loggers are undertaking land clearing with "no clues even on the method of felling in the development of an oil palm plantation" (email conversation, cf. Greenpeace, 2013b:5). Greenpeace documented ongoing clearings in November 2012 (Greenpeace, 2013a). This, as much as violations of the law cast doubt on the protection of its investors by the Zurich Insurance Political Risk Assurance which it claims to have obtained. This insurance scheme protects investors from expropriation, civil war, the cancellation of permits and other events that could harm a project. As a matter of fact, but for its 2,500ha pilot oil project in Ghana initiated in 2008, Herakles has limited experience in the development of a sustainable palm oil project. Internal memos attest to Herakles Farms telling investors of immediate profit uplift from the sale of timber, estimated to generate between $60 and 90 million, during the final phase of the project, until revenue from palm oil begins to flow in the later phases. Curiously enough, Herakles is neither an accredited commercial logging nor a timber trading company in Cameroon. These corporate misrepresentations put to question "the viability of the short-term revenue structure communicated to investors." This includes overreliance on the sale of harvested timber while planted oil palm mature (Greenpeace, 2013b:2).

Outright Disrespect of Restraining Court Orders

Apart from failing to file a counter affidavit, Herakles Farms snubbed a Court Order obtained by SEFE representing the local communities. The order restrained Herakles, and its agents and representatives from proceeding with the establishment of its oil palm plantation on grounds that the area is "national land," that the community lacks the "requisite locus standi to pursue it"[9] as well as the fact that in tandem with Article 1 of the 1974 Land Tenure Ordinance of the Republic of Cameroon (on rules governing land tenure," the plaintiffs/applicants ought to push the administration "to cause the Defendant/Respondents to comply with environmental requirements of land acquisition and not legal action in Court"[10]. This lack of consultation of locals and the subsequent demarcation of their land without free, prior, informed consent of communities that would be most affected has been decried by the transnational network of civil society activists (see also International Finance Corporation, 2012). Even Chief Atem Ebako of Talangaye, a lackey of the Yaounde regime is alleged to have "surrendered" 60 hectares of his personal land for trial nurseries and for the planting of oil palm. Though a Chief, and a member of the ruling CPDM party and therefore subservient to state, his action is at odds with Cameroon law as only the president is statutorily mandated to sign lease agreements of above 50 hectares. Although Herakles has so far failed to comply with three of the Court's orders (2, 3, 4) of 27/2/2012 (SUIT NO HCN/03/0S/2011), the Court curiously said they had complied by:

2. Compensating those directly affected by their farms and village settlements on the basis of the relevant law which is the Prime Ministerial text on the subject.

3. Compensating those affected by taking of their ancestral possessory rights over the land.

---

[9] The doctrine of locus standi in the area of human rights has been abolished by the Fundamental Rights (Enforcement Procedure) Rules 2009 which came into force on December 1, 2009.

[10] http://business-humanrights.org/sites/default/files/media/annex-ndian-cameroon-court-ruling-31-aug-2012.pdf.

4. Reaching a clear understanding with the indigenous people by way of a memorandum of understanding for the project to avert any future conflicts. It is even provided in the concession agreement that the company may rely on the coercive force of the state to remove people who refuse to move voluntarily[11,12].

Lack of Memorandum of Understanding (MOU) and Non-Respect of Initial Proposed Concession Boundary

Contrary to claims no MOU has been reached with each village whose land has been forcefully appropriated. Only two MoUs were allegedly signed by the people of the Nguti segment of the project and the other for the Mundemba and Toko Sub Divisions which amounts to invalid contracts. In Fabe, locals feel their chief betrayed and let them by the nose into accepting the establishment of the Herakles nursery. They revolted by blocking entry/roads to the nursery, and placed traditional fetishes as injunction. The regional Governor's visit to Toko Sub Division of June 6, 2012 was greeted with peaceful demonstration, anti-oil palm banners, T-shirts and placards by activists of the NGO SEFE.

Furthermore, the company is increasingly negotiating land in areas not covered by its ESIA. This is the case with the Mosongiseli and Ngumu blocks (11000ha). It is feared that its action will trigger land use conflicts/resource use conflicts between community members and neighboring communities. Social conflicts and a litany of human rights violations including expropriation of land from neighboring communities have already been reported in the area and will accentuate as the plantation expands (see also Cernea and Schmidt-Soltau, 2006, Brockington, 2002, Dunn, 2009, Igoe, 2004). This is happening against the backdrop of intense competition for more land in the community by the already established agro-industrial complexes-PAMOL and CDC. This looks like a sign of land 'speculation' starting in the area. The company is presently negotiating plantation blocks with Talangaye, Ekita, Ebanga and Menyamen and simultaneously opening the first 2500 ha plantation block. An

11 http://www.freundeskreis-partnerschaft-uebersee.de/uploads/media/UrteilMundemba 270212.pdf.

12 http://www.business-humanrights.org/media/annex-ndian-cameroon-court-ruling-31-aug-2012.pdf.

estimated 600ha of this block falls outside its proposed concession limit covered by their ESIA (Dupuy and Achankap, 2013). Even in instances where "negotiations" took place, neighbouring villages (Badun and New Konye) were sidelined in the negotiation process whereas the first block overlaps with their traditional ancestral land. Compounding the situation is the fact that plantation blocks are being clearly established within a rich secondary productive forest. Some 57000m3 of exploitable forest were inventoried within the 2500ha block. This is comparable to the volume that could be found in any other Forest Management Unit (FMU) exploited in the Southwest Region (Dupuy and Achankap, Ibid). There is clearly the non-respect of the so-called "Kupe and Ndian blocks" as the company is increasingly negotiating land in areas uncovered by its ESIA as well as huge expanse of land completely outside their planned concession around-Mosongisele, Weke, Idibanyanga and Ngumu. A total of 11000ha has been negotiated with these villages located just at the periphery of the KNP. In the Kupe-Muanenguba, the company is presently negotiating with the Upper Balong, Bassosi and Bakossi communities. It has signed MoUs with Talangaye, Ekita, Sikam, Simbaliba, Mayemen and Ebanga villages. The neighbouring villages of-Betock, Badun, New Konye, Mungo, Ndor, Bombe Konye and Ntale have adamantly refused to enter into any negotiation for land. These villages that are located on the Kumba-Mamfe road axis-a road of great economic importance, now being tarred claimed that they have an alternative vision of development for their communities.

Although the company has signed MOUs for 3,147ha with Manyemen and Ebanga villages, Betock village found within the area under negotiation was uninvolved in the exercise. Other MOUs have been signed with Sikam for 4500ha and with Sambaliba for 1000ha of their most fertile land and these villages are left with marginal lands and have requested to renegotiate with the company. The company has however faced spirited opposition in Ndian from the Meangwe, Mokange and Ndiba communities. By negotiating huge expanse of land around Mosongisele (8000ha), Weke, Idabanyanga and Ngumu (3000ha)- at the direct periphery of the KNP, local communities are left only with 3km peripheral zone to the park. This endangers/poses a direct threat to the KNP. The project is now overlapping with 3km peripheral zone of the KNP which had been excluded from the initial concession.

Additionally, as could be observed and as corroborated by NGO activists, after vigorous opposition from the inhabitants of Fabe village in Mundemba, Ndian Division where it started its first nursery Herakles is increasingly shifting its plantation development activities towards Nguti thereby illegally extending into lands that are not part of its concession. Rumours even have it that the company is planning to sell off its nurseries to Pamol which already has an established presence in the region. Such plans to sell nurseries and plantations to interested investors come 2017 would completely extinguish the indigenous community's hopes of regaining possession. The case of the CDC lands pitting the government and Cameroon and the Bakweri ethnic group when the company was privatized epitomises this (see Pemunta and Fonmboh, 2010).

Negative Environmental Consequences on Soils

The negative environmental consequences of the Herakles project include heightened erosion potential on steep slopes, and water quality (palm oil mill effluent/pollution by pesticide run-off). Furthermore, Green House Gas (GHG) emissions from land-use conversion are a major source of climate emissions. But even in the absence of land-use change methane emissions (from mill waste) are another potentially negative aspect, representing approximately 70% of total emissions from the operation of a plantation and mill, which can be problematic in the absence of digesters (see Hoyle and Levang, 2012:9). The project seriously threatens biodiversity conservation in the five protected areas within its borders, will produce millions of tons of GHG emissions and will also lead to millions of hectares of deforestation (Greenpeace, 2013a,b) as well as on non-forest products.

Increased Migration and Depletion of Resources

The establishment of the plantation will also orchestrate a huge and unprecedented influx of migrant workers to the area. As evidenced by the setting up of plantation agriculture in the fertile coastal areas of Southwest Cameroon by the German colonial administration (Pemunta and Fonmboh, 2010), it will intensify competition over farmlands and exacerbate the problem of climate change. The migration of migrant workers into the area will subsequently increase pressure on wildlife through hunting for the supply of bush meat-a much cherished delicacy in the area (see also Hoyle and Levang, 2012:9).

SUPPRESSION OF FOREST RESOURCES

The local communities are capable of obtaining more money with the Reduced Emissions from Deforestation and Degradation mechanism (REDD+) than the peanuts they have negotiated with the company. Moreover, with REDD+, they will still return their customary rights as well as reap benefits for environmental services provided by the forest. The state of Cameroon is being penny wise and pound foolish in allowing the conversion of forested land for palm oil production. The initial establishment contract showed that Herakles was to pay a land tax of 0.5 dollars per undeveloped ha against 1 dollar for developed ha/per year. This, as well as the "revised" versions are far too low when compared to exploitative timber exploitation whose concessionaires pay an average land tax of USD 5.0 per hectare per year, (and some as high as USD16) (MINFOF MINFI, 2010, cf Hoyle and Levang, 2012:11). By allowing the conversion of forest for palm oil production, the GoC is sacrificing alternative revenue sources from other land-use options-logging, mining, hunting, the collection of non-timber forest products (NTFP), conservation concession payments, and environmental services including ecotourism and REED+. These foregone activities can generate far more revenue to the state, local councils and local communities in tandem with the provisions of Cameroon's 1994 Forestry Law.

Most of Herakles's corporate defensive declarations including their claim that they are converting an area of little conservation value are economical of the truth and have been gainsaid by research findings. Research conducted by the University of Dschang in partnership with the University of Gőttingen and supported by Greenpeace International, SAVE Wildlife and WWF Germany branded that claim as a "severe misrepresentation" (http://www.save-wildlife.com/en/news).

The area provides habitat to chimpanzees, forest elephants, rare primates including-endangered drill, critically endangered preuss's red colobus monkey as well as myriad indigenous fish species. The concession area occupied by about 56 villages with a total population of about 16,000 inhabitants is an ecologically vital zone. Plantation development will lead to fragmentation of the landscape and to the total isolation of the surrounding protected areas (Dupuy and Achankap, 2013).

Lack of Negotiation

"Negotiation" is coercive, often comprised of 'intimidation and bribery, targeting chiefs and some influential members of the community.' In his theory of hegemony, Gramsci posited that the powerful maintain their power through a combination of coercion and consent which as a continuum serve to reinforce existing power structures. Those who oppose these structures by speaking truth to power are criminalized and punished accordingly. Local NGO activists including Nasako Besingi and his NGO, Struggle to Economise Future Environment (SEFE), working to protect people's rights and preserve forests in the area where Herakles is operating have severally been subjected to intimidation, lawsuits, arrests, and violent attacks. On December 31, 2013 Nasako was summoned, at the request of Herakles Farms, for "defamation." The crux of the matter is that in August 2012 Nasako was ambushed by a group of men that he identified as junior managers of Herakles Farms. Luckily he was being trailed by a team of French journalists from France24. Upon sighting their truck, the men let Nasako go and fled. Herakles Farms admitted that the men who attacked Nasako were "local service providers." Nasako and 4 colleagues are also facing other charges for organising "an undeclared public meeting" while distributing anti-Herakles t-shirts to locals[13]. On 3 November 2015, he was handed a heavy sentence: a fine of 1 million CFA Francs (1500 Euros) or 3 years imprisonment. He was also ordered to pay damages of 10 million CFA Francs (15000 Euros) to the two civil parties and costs of about 200,000 CFA Francs (300Euros). He was given 24 hours to pay the amount of the fine[14].

'At their fundamental levels,' the 'dual perspective' correspond to the 'dual nature' of Machiavelli's Centaur-half animal and half-human.' These for Gramsci are 'the levels of force and consent, domination and hegemony, violence and civilisation' (Gramsci, 1971:169-70). Similarly Fontana (2006:43) argues that power is dualistic-comprising 'force and consent, violence and persuasion.' Jessop's (2007:241) Gramsci-inspired continuum of hegemony, passive revolution, force-fraud-corruption…are also possible forms of domination. Gramsci (1971:156) further surmised that class power could operate in ways other than coercion and consent: "Between consent and force stands corruption-fraud... that is, the procurement of the antagonists'

[13] http://wrm.org.uy/all-campaigns/your-support-is-needed-cameroon-activists-on-trial-for-peaceful-protest-against-wall-street-land-grabber/

[14] http://business-humanrights.org/en/nasako-besingi-director-of-a-leading-environmental-ngo-heavily-sentenced-for-fighting-the-injustice-of-land-grabs-in-the-south-west-of-cameroon.

debilitation and paralysis by buying...their leaders. ...” The negotiation process is opaque, characterized by multiple double standards-it further differs from one village to the other. The negotiation contradict the core principle of “Free, Prior and Informed Consent” (FPIC principles)-“FPIC implies that communities have the right to decide whether they will agree to the project or not once they have a full and accurate understanding of the implications of the project on them and their customary land”[15,16].

The Herakles land negotiation process consists of 1) The production of a “participatory sketch map” of the area outlining sacred sites, farm lands, settlements, protected areas and communal land (“unused land”) on the maps endorsed by the village chiefs representing traditional councils and thereafter by local administrative officials. 2) Field surveys geo-referencing land use type 3) Negotiation sessions with the villages and the signing of MOUs during which communities are convinced to part with as much land as possible, without any care for neither their present welfare nor their future development needs.

Local communities do not master the technicalities of land use mapping and land negotiation processes. This explains their later realization and the need to renegotiate. Their myopia is further attested by the vague and oftentimes, elusive language embedded in the MOUs 1) “SGSOC will leave out land for local out grower schemes for the cultivation of palm oil and purchase the resulting [products] thereby providing a credit-worthy reliable buyer for local farmer’s production” (surface to be used is not mentioned as well as the schedule, finance and technical support). 2) “SGSOC will produce electricity and where practicable will make surplus available to the communities at low cost.” 3) “SGSOC will create long-term employment” (even when most plantation jobs are seasonal, for whom, how many, for how long?, what qualifications?”) (Dupuy and Achankap, 2013:6-7, see also cameroonveritas.files.wordpress.com/2011/12).

Various promises such as those to provision two classrooms, community hall, roads and water, are in fact, tools for the production of capital. These are incentives to ensure the company’s implantation in the area. For example, roads will serve in the development of their plantation, electricity and water will ensure their production, classrooms will keep workers on the site. Even more interesting is the fact that there are variations from one village to the other in terms of annual compensation. Whereas the MOU states that “SGSOC

[15] See also http://www.hcvnetwork.org/news-and-events/2013_heraklesletter.

[16] http://www.forestpeoples.org/guiding-principles/free-prior-and-informed-consent-fpic.

will contribute a monthly stipend of 50,000FCFA per month beginning from the first year of operation and 200000FCFA per month from the start of production," some villages have been able to obtain on paper 200 000FCFA for the chiefdom and 400000FCFA for the village per month (Dupuy and Achankap, 2013:7).

CORRUPT BUSINESS PRACTICES

Greenpeace (2013b:4) cites a Herakles Farms employee as asserting "... of course, envelopes were distributed [...] that is how you facilitate your way." The same insider source further hinted that a former plantation Director "distributed a good number of envelopes and huge sums of money" (Ibid). This resonates with the declarations of several respondents who maintained that "lips were oiled," "palms were held with something," "huge envelopes changed hands." The Cameroon Ministry of Forestry and Wildlife Programme for the Sustainable Management of Natural Resources (PSMNR) collected information from 20 villages and mentions "... a lot of intimidation and bribery targeting the chiefs and some few influential decision making members of the communities"[17] (see also Dupuy and Achankap, 2013:7). Two Cameroonian NGOs, the Center for Environment and Development (CED) and the Network to Fight Against Hunger (RELUFA) filed a complaint with the American Government via its National Contact Point for the Organisation for Economic Cooperation and Development (OECD) concerning these allegations of corruption. This shows the collusion of political elites as well as their subversion of the state in their pursuit of personal interests (Chabal and Deloz, 1999, 2006). Similarly, Bayart et al., (1998) have demonstrated how the predatory activities of elites tend to 'criminalize' and undermine the state while they enrich themselves through corruption and misrule. Extrapolating insights from the neo-patrimonial perspective, William Reno demonstrates how external actors impact on local neo-patrimonial networks and the political elites in Africa through kickbacks. By construction 'shadow states' and 'shadow economies,' they significantly undermine formal state and economic structures by engaging in profitable informal economic activities from which they reap direct profits at the detriment of the state or people leading to feelings of acrimony, violence and predatory behavior (Reno, 2000, see also

[17] http://www.relufa.org/documents/pressrelease.pdf.

Obi, 2009:110-111). This shows the co-existence of the legal and the illegal economy (see also Bennafla, 2013, Kopytoff 1987a,b).

Greenpeace (2013b) has severally documented the major shortcomings of the Herakles project as well as the questionable tactics deployed to make it look sustainable and beneficial to Cameroon (see also Oakland Institute and Greenpeace, 2012). Following Greenpeace, internal company communication attests to deceit towards investors, local communities, the state of Cameroon and the general public about the status and operations of Herakles project in the country: "significant discrepancies between how the company has represented the project to the public and what it is telling prospective investors...internal communications that contradict the optimistic outlook for the palm oil project presented to investors."

1) Contrary to public statements to stakeholders that all the necessary permits and approvals had been secured to proceed with field operations, this had not been done. A presidential decree granting a temporary concession was only signed on November 25, 2013 ceding 19,843 hectares for three years renewable depending on their ability to respect engagements. This is happening after Herakles Farms has been operating in illegality for four years[18] (2) breach of 1976 Cameroonian law governing the allocation of land concessions on state lands which require that a presidential decree be obtained for any concession above 50 ha. Even more troublesome is the fact that even without exonerating Herakles from obtaining necessary permits-including a land lease prior to exercising rights- the 2009 Convention was [until recently] still invalidated by the president (Greenpeace, 2013b:1).

Herakles's actions have been characterized by unethical and dubious business practices. The company started the development of palm nurseries in 2010 prior to undertaking the required ESIA, neither securing land lease nor obtaining consent from impacted communities, still to secure widespread consent and instead faces stiff resistance from several village communities. Various violations of Cameroonian law have met with several court cases and project delays that do not come cheap. For example, illegal logging and lack of proper authorization led to its being hit with a fine of 45 000USD. Accusations of failure to respect national and international standards in the establishment of its plantation pushed Herakles Farms into withdrawing an application for membership of the Kuala Lumpur-based RSPO in August of 2012. The certification body was created in 2004 to help palm oil producers, in part,

[18] http://bongben.wordpress.com/2013/11/27/cameroon-grants-land-lease-to-sgsoc-despite - protests/.

improve their reputation following a barrage of claims they were orchestrating irrevocable damage to forests and to wildlife. RSPO also seeks to increase palm oil producers' access especially to US and European markets while shoring up access to investor capital and improving ties with communities where they operate and their workers.

Herakles's actions have been characterized by unethical and dubious business practices. The company started the development of palm nurseries in 2010 prior to undertaking the required ESIA. Furthermore, it neither secured a land lease nor obtained consent from impacted communities. Various violations of Cameroonian law have met with several court cases and project delays that do not come cheap. For example, illegal logging and lack of proper authorization led to its being hit with a fine of 45 000USD. Accusations of failure to respect national and international standards in the establishment of its plantation pushed Herakles Farms into withdrawing an application for membership of the Kuala Lumpur-based Roundtable on Sustainable Palm Oil (RSPO) in August of 2012. This certification body was created in 2004 to help palm oil producers, in part, to improve their reputation following a barrage of claims they were orchestrating irrevocable damage to forests and to wildlife. RSPO also seeks to increase palm oil producers' access especially to US and European markets while shoring up access to investor capital and improving ties with communities where they operate and their workers.

CONCLUSION

In the face of the intractable problem of climate change, the United Nations appointed World Commission on Environment and Development ('Brundtland Commission') declared that "one of the most serious threats to our civilisation is the accelerating deterioration of our environment." In its proposed blueprint for a synergy between the environment and development, the Commission stated that development should "meet the needs of the present without compromising the ability of future generations to meet their own needs." Its "overall assessment" called for a synergy and new model between the imperatives of the environment and development: "the international economy must speed up world growth while respecting environmental constraints" (World Commission on Environment and Development (WCED), 1987). It has been widely recognized that "we must not succumb to the temptation to put the environment in one category and development in another, or imagine that policy dealing with one does not deal with the other" (Hawke,

1989:1). The cross-road between the environment and corporate profit by the State-Herakles alliance eloquently demonstrates the disentanglement of sustainability and development as encapsulated in the setting up of this plantation complex in the evergreen forest of Southwest Cameroon without the prior, informed consent of the local communities inhabiting the area. This is the case because "agricultural policies clearly lie at the root of land, water, and forest degradation" (WCED, 1987).

In the process of territorialization which involves the creation/expansion of protected areas, internal state and non-state forces/actors collude and exploit locals. The conjuncture between neoliberal governance and fortress conservation does not bode well for the environment. Enclosures and associated changes in social relations are dangerous to conservation as locals often protest against lost commons in both overt and covert ways. This often results in secret, widespread and unsustainable use of protected areas by local inhabitants for agriculture; grazing, timber exploitation and hunting (see Kelly, 2011:695, Cernea and Schmidt-Soltau, 2006). They have lost any sense of local ownership and lack the incentive to protect the environment. They are resisting 'official' discourses of state, sovereignty, and human-nature relationships in myriad ways (Brockington, 2002, Dunn, 2009, Igoe, 2004). As one respondent maintained:

> We have suddenly become thieves on our own land and forest. After chasing us away in the name of conservation and now plantation agriculture, we have been harvesting whatever we need as thieves do since we could be arrested and fined or gunned down by park guards (Nkongho, Interview of November 20, 2010).

The Herakles Farms case study exposes various territorial strategies deployed by the state in shaping particular territories into monocultures of oil palm for biofuels. The state and its agents deploy the discursive repertoires of capitalist development "designed to shape and reshape territorial spaces into nationalized, nationalizing unities within a broader context defined by "the world market" (Brenner and Elden, 2009:363). In other words, territorialized organization of governance continues to be a significant force under capitalist production, where economic processes materialize territorially into state policies (Brenner 1999, Harvey, 2003). This is achieved independent of the will of the local community inhabiting the area given the state's monopoly over all parcels of land as well as symbolic violence. The state's policies and legal templates crafted in tune with the colonial era-in the name of market integration and civilization delineate and enforce the agribusiness project and serves as a facilitative regime (see Harvey, 2010, 2006). Another mechanism for the achievement of its hegemonic project is the use of coercion and force. State policies and discourses of representation tend to facilitate land grabs, and not only consent, but also violence and terror have been effective tools for land dispossession and social control (see also Martinez, 2011:54, Lefebre, 1991). Violence is often clothed in rationality-as captured by the metaphors of progress and development, and rationality is deployed as justification for violence (Lefebre, 1991:280-281). The Cameroon government's territorial production has led to the present day conundrum of Ndian Division as a site bereft of, and where development has instead been transformed into underdevelopment. People are now seen as standing in the way of "progress"-(capitalist development)- be it large-scale agricultural development or conservation of protected areas which is meant to benefit outsiders, while leaving behind broken livelihoods.

The government of Cameroon needs to re-orientate the present institutional architecture in which the state claims monopoly over land and other mineral resources, recognize community land tenure and ownership so as to improve the socioeconomic livelihood of local communities. An institutional adjustment will empower local communities to negotiate with investors on their own terms.

REFERENCES

African Development Bank. (2009). Cameroon Diagnostic Study for Modernization of the Lands and Survey Sectors. Country Regional Centre (ORCE).

Anderson, P. (2011). The antinomies of Antonio Gramsci, 5-78, *New Left Review*, 1/100, Nov-Dec.

Anyangwe, C. (1987). *The Cameroonian Judicial System*. Yaounde: CEPER.

Ayim, M. A. (2008). *Former British Southern Cameroons Journey towards Complete Decolonization, Independence and Sovereignty. A Comprehensive Compilation of Efforts and Historical Documentation.* Bloomington: Author House.

Bennafla, K. (2013). Contemporary transnational circulation of goods in Africa:A form of legitimation of State borders. *Locus: revista de historia*, juiz de Fora, v.18, no2p. 215-234.

Buchs, T. D. (2003). Privatization in Sub-Saharan Africa: Some Lessons from Experiences to date. Available http://ideas.repec.org/p/wpa/wuwpmi/0502007. html. Accessed December 5, 2013.

Ciccantell, P and Smith, D. A. (2009). Rethinking Global Commodity Chains: Integrating Extraction, Transport, and Manufacturing. *International Journal of Comparative Sociology*, Vol.50(3-4):361-384.

Collier, P and Hoeffer, A. (2000). Greed and grievance in civil wars, World Bank policy Research. Working Paper No.2355, available at SSRN: http://ssrn.com/abstract=630. Accessed December 5, 2013.

Dupuy, J, and Achankap, B. M. (2013). Report of Fact finding Mission on Herakles Farms (SGSOC) oil palm plantation project, February, November 4.

Dunn, KC. Contested State Spaces: African National Parks and the State. *European Journal of International Relations*, Vol.15(3):423-446.

Escobar, A. (2008). *Termites of Difference: Place, Movements, Life, Redes.* Durham: Duke University Press.

Fisiy, C. F. (1992). *Power and Privilege in the Administration of Law: Land Law Reforms and Social Differentiation in Cameroon.* Leiden: African Studies Centre.

Fontana, B. (2006). Liberty and Domination: Civil Society in Gramsci. *Boundary*, 2 33, no. 2:51-74.

Forrest, J. B. (1988). The quest for State 'Hardness' in Africa. *Comparative Politics*, Vol, 20(4):423-442.

Geary, K. (2012). *'Our Land, Our Lives': Time out on the global land rush.* London: Oxfam.

Gill, S. (2000). "Knowledge, Politics, and Neo-Liberal Political Economy," in: R. Stubbs, and G. Underhill (eds). *Political Economy and the Changing Global Order*, (p. 48-59, Oxford: Oxford University Press.

Gramsci, A. (1971). *Selections from the Prison Notebooks of Antonio Gramsci.* New York: International Publishers.

Greenpeace. (2013a). Herakles Farms in Cameroon. A Showcase of palm oil production. Washington DC. Greenpeace.

Greenpeace. (2013b). Herakles Exposed:The truth behind Herakles Farms false promises in Cameroon. Available http://www.greenpeace.org/international/Global/international/
briefings/forests/2013/Herakles_ExposedFinal.pdf (accessed November, 04, 2013).

Government of Cameroon. (GoC). (2009). Growth and Employment Strategy Paper (GESP). Reference Framework for Government Action over the period 2010-2020. Washington, DC: International Monetary Fund.

GoC. (1974a). Ordonnance No. 74-1 du juillet 1974 fixant regime foncier. http://camerounforet.com/system/files/18_93_99.pdf. (Accessed 15 July 2013).

GoC. (1974b). Ordonnance No. 74-2 du juillet 1974 fixant le regime domanial. http://camerounforet. com/system/files/18_93_99.pdf (accessed 15 July 2013).

Hale, C. (2005). "Neoliberal Multiculturalism: The remaking of Cultural rights and racial dominance in Central America," *Political and Legal Anthropology Review*, Vol.28, No.1, pp.10-28.

Harvey, D. (2010). *The Enigma of Capital and the Crises of Capitalism*. London: Profile Books Ltd.

Harvey, D. (2006). *Limits to Capital*. London: New York:Verso.

Harvey, D. (2003). *The New Imperialism*: Oxford: Oxford University Press.

Hawke, R.J.L. (1989). 'The Challenge to the Mining Industry,' *Mining Review*, (2), 1-9.

Hédin, L. 1930. Étude sur la forêt et les bois du Cameroun sous mandat française. Librairie Larose, Paris, France.

High Conservation Value Resource Network (HCV). (2012). HCV Resource Network Technical Panel Peer Review of Assessment of High Conservation Value on the SGSOC Concession for Oil Palm Development in Southwestern Cameroon. Available http://www.hcvnetwork.org/resources/assessments/SGSOC%20review_HCV%20TP_full%20final%20public.pdf. (Accessed December 5, 2013).

International Finance Corporation (IFC). (2007). Stakeholder Engagement: A Good Practice Handbook for Companies Doing Business in Emerging Markets. Washington: World Bank Group.

International Finance Corporation (IFC). (2012). Performance Standards on Environmental and Social Sustainability. Washington: World Bank Group. Available http://www.ifc.org/wps/wcm/connect/115482804a0255db96fbffd1a5d13d27/PS_English_2012_Full-Document.pdf?MOD=AJPERES (January 3, 2014).

Kamphorst, B. (1994). A socio-economic study on the distribution and marketing pattern of marine fish products in Ndian Division, South West Province, Republic of Cameroon. Technical Report No.62. Cotonou. Food and Agriculture Organization of the United Nations.

Kelly, A. B. (2011). Conservation practice as primitive accumulation, *The Journal of Peasant Studies*, Vol. 38:4,683-701.

Konings, P. (2011). 'agro-industry and regionalism in the South West Province of Cameroon during the National Economic and Political Crisis,'

Nkwi, P. N, and Nyamnjoh, F. B. (eds).(2011). *Regional Balance and National Integration in Cameroon. Lessons Learned and the Uncertain Future*, (pp. 505-517). Bamenda: Langaa Research and Publishing Common Initiative Group.

Letouzey, R. (1957). La forêt à Lophira alata de la zone littorale Camerounaise. Bois et Forêt des Tropiques 53:9–20.

Le Vine, VT. (1964). *The Cameroons: From Mandate to Independence*. Berkeley: University of California Press.

Lefebvre, H. (1991). *State, Space, World: Selected Essays*. Edited by Stuart Elden and Neil Brenner. Minneapolis, MN:University of Minnesota Press.

Lefebvre, H. (1988). *The Production of Space*. Oxford: Willey-Blackwell.

Li, T. (2011). "Centering Labor in the land grab debate." *The Journal of Peasant Studies*, 38(2):281-99.

Martinez, A.M.R. (2011). Contemporary Land grabbing in Colombia: The role of the state, ethnicity and violence. A Research paper in partial fulfillment of the requirements for obtaining the degree of Masters of Arts in Development Studies (Government and Democracy). The Hague: The Netherlands.

Marcus, G. E. (1995). Ethnography in/of the World System: The Emergence of Mult-Sited Ethnography. *Annual Review of Anthropology*. Vol. 24: 95-117.

Mentan, T. (2011). 'The Political Economy of Regional Imbalances and National "Unintegration" in Cameroon,' P. N Nkwi, and F. B, Nyamnjoh (eds). *Regional Balance and National Integration in Cameroon. Lessons Learned and the Uncertain Future*, (pp.19-40). Bamenda:Langaa Research and Publishing Common Initiative Group.

Moritz, M. (2006). The politics of permanent conflict: Farmer-Herder conflicts in Northern Cameroon. *Canadian Journal of African Studies*, 40, 1:101-126.

Nkwi, P. N, and Nyamnjoh, F. B. (eds). *Regional Balance and National Integration in Cameroon. Lessons Learned and the Uncertain Future*. Bamenda:Langaa Research and Publishing Common Initiative Group.

Nnoli, O. N. (1980). *Ethnic Politics in Nigeria*. Enugu: Fourth Dimension Publishers.

Noorduyn, R. E. (2005). The assertion of rights to agro-pastoral land in North Cameroon: a cascade to violence? Ph.D Dissertation, Faculty of Social and Behavioural Sciences. University of Amsterdam.

Obi, C. (2009). Nigeria's Niger Delta: Understanding the Complex Drivers of Violent Oil-related Conflict. *Africa Development,* Vol. XXXIV, No. 2, 2009, pp. 103–128.

Oakland Institute. (2012). Understanding Land Investment Deals in Africa, Massive Deforestation Portrayed as Sustainable Development: the Deceit of Herakles Farms in Cameroon, Land Deal Brief, September 2012, http://www.oaklandinstitute.org/land-deals-africa-cameroon. (Accessed October 20, 2013).

Peluso, N. L. and Lund, C. (2011). New frontiers of land control: Introduction. *Journal of Peasant Studies*, 38(4), 667–681.

Peluso, N. L. and Lund, C, (eds). (2011). New frontiers of land control. Special Issue, *Journal of Peasant Studies*, 38(4), 667–681.

Peluso, N. and Vandergeest, P. (2011). "Political ecologies of war and forest: Counterinsurgencies and the making of national natures,"*Annals of the Association of American Geographers*, 101:3,587-608.

Pemunta, N. V. (2014). New Forms of Land Enclosures: Multinationals and State production of territory in Cameroon. *STUDIA UBB SOCIOLOGIA, LIX*, 2, pp. 35-58.

Pemunta, N. V, Aristide, A. B. (2013). Socio-spatial occupation, conflict and humanitarian assistance for Bororo cross-border migrants in east Cameroon. *International Journal of Development Issues*, Vol. 12, 3: pp. 271 – 288.

Pemunta, N. V, and Mbu-Arrey, O. P. (2013). The tragedy of the governmentality of nature: the case of national parks in Cameroon, in J. B, Smith (ed). *National Parks: Sustainable Development, Conservation Strategies and Environmental Impacts*. (p. 1-46), New York: Nova Science Publishers Inc. ISBN: 978-1-62618-935-5.

Pemunta, N. V. (2013). The governance of nature as development and the erasure of the Pygmies of Cameroon. *GeoJournal*, 78,2: 353 - 371. ISSN: 0343-2521 DOI: 10.1007/s10708-011-9441-7.

Pemunta, N. V. and Fonmboh, N. M. (2010). "Experiencing Neoliberalism from below: The Bakweri Confrontation of the State of Cameroon over the Privatization of the Cameroon Development Corporation." *Journal of Human Security*, 6, 38-53.

Peters, P. E. (2004). Inequality and social conflict over land in Africa. *Journal of Agrarian Change*, 4, 3, 269 -314.

Richards, M. (2013). Social and Environmental Impacts of Agricultural Large-Scale Land Acquisitions in Africa-With a Focus on West and Central Africa. Washington, DC: Rights and Resource Initiative.

Roitman, J. (2007). The Right to Tax: Economic Citizenship in the Chad Basin, *Citizenship Studies,* 11:2, 187-209, DOI:10. 1080/1362102070 1262636.

Roitman, J. (2004). *Fiscal Disobedience: an anthropology of economic regulation in Central Africa*. Princeton: NJ: Princeton University Press.

Rubin, N. (1971*). Cameroun: An African Federation*. New York: Praeger.

Schmidt-Soltau, K. (2003). Conservation-related resettlement in Central Africa: environmental and social risks. *Development and Change*, 34(3),525-51.

Van De Walle, N. (1989). Privatization in Developing Countries: A Review of the Issues. *World Development*, Vol. 17(5):601-615.

Vandergeest, P. and Peluso, N. (1995). "Territorialization and State Power in Thailand." *Theory and Society*, 24(3):385-426.

World Bank. (2010). Rising global interests in farmland: can it yield sustainable and equitable benefits? Washington, DC: World Bank.

World Bank. (2003). Land policies for growth and poverty reduction. Washington, DC: World Bank.

Zoomers, A. (ed.). (2001). *Land and sustainable livelihood in Latin America.* Royal Tropical Institute, KIT Publishers, Amsterdam, The Netherlands. 257pp.

Zoomers, A. (2010). Globalisation and the foreignisation of space: seven processes driving the current global land grab. *Journal of Peasant Studies*, 37(2):429-47.

INDEX

D

E

F

G

H

I

J

K

L

M

N

O

P

Q

R

S

T

U

V

W

Y